A
MUSLIM
HUSBAND
AND
WIFE

Rights and Duties

Sabir Uddin

kitab bhavan
New Delhi-110 002

KITAB BHAVAN
Exporters & Importers
1784, Kalan Mahal, Daryaganj
New Delhi-110002, [India]

Phones : 3274686, 3277392, 3277393
Fax   : 91-11-3263383
Telex   : 31-63106 ALI IN

First Edition   1990
Third Edition 1997
Fourth Edition 2000

ISBN 81-7151-112-0

Published by:
Nusrat Ali Nasri for Kitab Bhavan
1784, Kalan Mahal, Daryaganj
New Delhi-110002

Laser Type Setting at:
Laser Track
1784, Kalan Mahal, Daryaganj
New Delhi - 110002

Printed in India at:
Lahooti Fine Art Press
1711, Sui Walan, Darya Ganj,
New Delhi - 110002 (India)
Tel. : 3286349

CONTENTS

INTRODUCTION

Before discussing the rights and duties of a Muslim husband and wife in the light of the *Qur'an* and the *Hadiths*, it is necessary to have a glimpse of the situation prevailing in the Arab world before the advent of the Holy Prophet Mohammad (peace be on him and his progeny). The country was divided into tribes. The tribal chiefs were selected for their physical prowess and ability to control the people. It was "Might prevailing over right". Consequently, the weak were at the mercy of the strong. It goes without saying that where such a situation prevails, corruption is bound to be rampant there. In most clans, the chiefs were elected on account of their nobility of birth, wisdom or courage. There were no regular laws, & no machinery for justice to be carried out. Idolatory prevailed over the entire Arabian peninsula. Religion and morality had been relegated to the past. Polygamy was popular *trait*. Divorce was very easy and at the whim of the husband. Female infanicide was also common. Women had no legal rights, and were treated worse than animals. They were regarded as a plaything of the males. Adultery, fornication and debauchery was the order of the day.

In fact, laws the world over at that time had deprived women of their rights. Manu's law in India recognised her as a means of procreation, and the aim of her life was to entertain and serve the master to the maximum and die while serving him. She had no place in social life. Christianity, on the other hand, was of the view that men and the women cannot be treated at par. The man only was considered to be a human, and not the woman. Roman Law, which is the fountain-head or the nucleus of all wordly laws, too could not equalise her with man. In social life, father, brothers, husband, and sons had definite places, but the wife had no place at all. The word "human" meant only the man. Woman could stand under the shadow of her man, but could not stand with him on the same platform. The Jews called woman "A born sin" as she was considered to be responsible for the exit of Adam from Heaven.

It is only the Qur'an, which not only recognised the rights of women, but gave her an equal status with men. *"Wala-hunna Misslil Lazi Alaihin Bil Moroof"*. (2:228) (The wife too has the same rights over the husband as the husband has over her)". These four words gave woman the rights which she was previously denied. It was the medieval age where the sword was the final arbiter of matters. People were mercifully slain on trifles. The time was ripe for emergence of a simple & rational faith like Islam. Islam first laid down concrete laws and ushered in the world a new era in human history where amongst other things women were given the same rights as men.

Islam is the last revealed religion. It is an Arabic word. And technically *means complete submission AND UNCONDITIONAL SURRENDER TO ALLAH,* Who has been sending His Prophet from time immemorial to ameliorate the world as a whole. Mohammed (Peace be on him and his Progeny) was His last Prophet. He identified himself as a simple human being sent by God to the earth as His Prophet, and not as a 'Son of God'.

Now the question arises as to who is a Muslim? Does a man inherit Islam (through his birth in a Muslim family)? Is he a Muslim merely due to the fact that his forefathers were Muslims ? Certainly not. *A Muslim is that - and only that who adopts Islam of his own accord, believes in oneness of God, through his strong faith in Him, in the Hereafter, in the unseen, in the angels, and firmly believes and confesses that the Prophet Mohammad (Peace be on him and his progeny) was his last Prophet, and maintains his belief as such till the end of his life.*

A person, irrespective of his caste, creed and

belief, is a Muslim if he accepts the tenets of Islam and gives them a practical shape in every sphere of life. Similarly, if a person, though born in a Muslim family, does not follow the *Qur'anic ways of life*, cannot be called a Muslim, though he may be the son of a Muslim. He must know his Lord and his relations with Him i.e. of "*Serf and the Lord*; know what his *Lord* wants or expects from him; which is the proper course for him to tread on in order to reach *His throne*; what pleases and displeases *Him*. After attaining such requisite qualifications he must unconditionally surrender to Him and not only obey, but try to propitiate Him by complying with His orders. He must abstain and refrain himself from indulging in what the Lord does not like. He must control himself and shed his based desires and be always ready to sacrifice everything for the sake of his *Lord*. It is also necessary that his faith must be unshakeable and he must adhere to it strictly till his last breath. Similarly, a person after embracing Islam, must understand thoroughly what he reads in the *Qur'an,* and practise them in real life.

It is thus clear that for a Muslim the first and foremost duty is the acquisition of education and knowledge, and then bringing it into practise, so that his actions, behaviour, manners and ways of life could reflect Islam in the real sense, and he, in turn could influence others with the spirit of Islam. The difference between a Muslim and non-Muslim is not that of nomenclature, but of presentation of character. A Muslim must be a man of an irreproachable integrity. He must be affluent with the wealth of unshakable faith & piety, undoubtful honesty & truth. His heart must be full of tremendous love and compassion for all. He must reflect the qualities of mutual respect, tolerance, resignation, fair-dealing & devotion to duty. He must be a package of virtues & a torch-bearer to humanity at large. Unless he knows what the *Qur'an* and the *Hadiths* say, he will not be able to present a true picture of his faith before the world. For a true Muslim what is needed is true understanding of the holy books and a life pattern that adheres to the teachings of the Qur'an and the Hadiths.

Some people feel that the Qur'an can be understood only by religious heads. It is a wrong notion. There are some, who for their own selfish ends try to misguide the people by stressing that they will not understand the Holy book. They do it to establish their hold over the masses. The Qur'an must be read and understood by all. Annotating the implied meanings of *Ayat No. 82 of Surah AN-NISA of the Holy Qur'an.* Maulana Abul Kalam Azad, in his "Tarjuman-ul-Qur'an", has said that the Holy Qur'an demands that everybody himself must give his own closed attention to understand it accurately, and the notion that it is for the Religious Heads to understand it, is not correct. Only those, who will try to understand it, will get its hidden meanings. It is like a traveller climbing a mountain; The higher he goes. the further he sees.

So far as the concept of the Holy Prophet (peace be on him and his progeny) regarding the acquisition of knowledge is concerned, he has clearly stressed time and again that a Muslim must acquire knowledge and education even if he has to travel to China. There is an incident where the Holy Prophet (Peace be on him and his progeny) promised the prisoners of war that they would be set free if they imparted education to the illiterate Muslims.

The *Qur'an* is a *Divine Book*, which is in *God's own words* as revealed to the Prophet Mohammed (peace be on him and his progeny). It is not like common books on metaphysics etc. based on mere speculations and conjectures. It is based on *Truth*, because its author *Allah* has full knowledge of the reality. After asserting this fact, there is no room left to doubt its contents. It verily showed the right path, and initiated man to the *Unseen*. It stressed upon man to have a firm belief in the *Hereafter*.

The Qur'an, in the present shape, is a complete record of revelations which dawned on the prophet (peace be on him and his progeny). Verses were revealed to the Prophet (peace be on him and his

---

China at that time was considered to be an inaccessable place.

progeny) from time to time, which were then scribbled on the material available in those days, such as palm-leaves, stones, skins of animals etc.

At the time of the death of the Holy (Prophet Peace be on him and his progeny) a good deal of the Qur'an was already written, though not all of it. Besides, the revealed verses were committed to memory by the *Noble Companions* of the Holy Prophet (Peace be on him and his progeny). During the life time of the Holy Prophet (Peace be on him and his progeny) new surahs (verses) or chapters were constantly being added to it, and after His death ;evelations came to an end, The same system of committing the *Holy Qur'an* to memory is still in vogue in order to preserve it with utmost accuracy; even with punctuations and if God wills, it will remain as such for ever. The Holy Prophet (Peace be on him and his progeny) used to pronounce legal decisions on the cases brought to him for decision in the light of the Qur'an. Above all, he used to sermonise His Companions from time to time. His pronouncements and sermons were called Hadiths. These were collected from far and wide. While collecting the sayings of the Holy Prophet (Peace be on him and his progeny) it was strictly kept in view that the narrator must be a True Muslim i.e. who fears *Allah*, discriminates between good and evil, and intends to be a righteous, God-fearing and Truth-loving human being. Most authentic Hadiths are called Sahih. The most trustworthy way of verifying their veracity was their corroboration by some other responsible and reliable Companion of the Prophet (Peace be on him and his progeny) who were present at the time of uttering the actual words. The scholars of Islamic studies sometimes had to undertake long journeys to collect actual words of the Prophet (Peace be on him and his progeny) from those who had heard them with their own ears.

The message of the, Holy Qur'an was accepted by the people gladly as it was socialistic and democratic in nature. Accumulation of wealth and worship of *Mammon* was forbidden. The *Qur'an* enjoined the Muslims to divide the property after one's death and to pay Zakat (obligatory alm) every year. The greatest characteristic of Islam is that the laws of governance are lucidly laid down in the religious texts.

The Prophet (Peace be on him and his progeny) never claimed that Islam is a new religion. According to Him, it has been existing from the very inception of the earth and has constantly been preached by the former Prophets (Peace be on them) from *Nuh to Mohammad* (Peace be on him and his progeny). In its present form, it will continue to exist till the last date of the world. The Prophet (Peace be on him and his progeny) discarded racial discrimination, mutual hatred, jealousy, and vanity. He Himself, in his last sermon to the Ummah has said, *"An Arab has no superiority over a non-Arab; and a non-Arab has no superiority over an Arab; except of course, that he excels the latter in piety. You are sons of Adam, and Adam was made of earth. God has removed from you the blemishes of ignorance and the pride of birth. Now, there are only two classes of men : those who are righteous & those who are wicked and sinful. Verily all Muslims are brothers "* In order to demonstrate the actual spirit of Islamic law, the Muslims have been enjoined to show generosity to all, and are asked to be freed from the bonds of meaness, selfishness, and peevishness of mind, as it is necessary pre-requisite for the *Ummah* throughout the world.

We have seen that the *Qur'an* and the Holy Prophet (Peace be on him and his progeny) in the face of pessimism, idolatory, and immorality, have wielded the torch of monotheism and morality. We can imagine how difficult the task must have been for those who established the *Kingdom of Allah,* obliterated the evils, and paved the way to *Heaven* for us. We must be grateful to the Almighty that He brought us to the world where we get the chance to look into the glorious text of *the Holy Qur'an*, and make it our mentor, guide and everything. It is, of course, our misfortune that the Devil has gripped and misled us and we, instead of seeking the redressal of our grievances in the *The Qur'an* and the *Hadiths,* wonder about in vain. In the words of Maulana Abul Kalam Azad: "We want to lit our lamp with the help of others light and have forgotton to trace out our own lost candle made of camphor, which once had illuminated the whole world. It is a pity that we look forward for others' theories to take help from, and neglect our own Divine Laws whose unparallel principals are applicable to everybody for all times. These are made of honey. & honey is always sweet-whether it is in the present or in future."

Through this book, my aim is to awaken the misguided people and the Muslims in particular and to remind them of their responsibilities towards the world at large. Islam has taught us tolerance, fortitude and perseverance and directed us to shun and discard hatred, prejudice and other social evils, to which the world in the pre-Islamic period was subjected. We can solve our contemporary problems howsoever insoluble they appear to be, if we turn to the Qur'an and Hadiths. Had we enough religious knowledge Shah Bano would not have gone to Supreme Court of India & the matter in the light of *Qur'an* & *Hadith* would have been decided before & mud-slinging would have been avoided.

I have tried my best to discuss the problems relating to husbands and wives as a whole, particularly for the youths of today, who, due to disenchantment or some odd circumstances have no time to study the laws of the *Shariah*. I hope that some of them atleast will take trouble to study this book carefully and minutely.

While writing this book I had to take recourse to some books for my ready reference and personal guidance. I have adopted the translated pieces of Qur'anic verses as such along with some pieces of commentary from the most renowned and authentic translations of The Holy Qur'an such as "The Meaning of the Qur'an by (late) Syed Abul A'la Maududi, "The meaning of the Glorious Qur'an " by Allama Abdullah Yusuf Ali," The Tarjuman-ul-Qur'an" by Maulana Abul Kalam Azad & "Relations of Peace" by Dr. S.M.Iqbal, Safina-e-Nijat by Maulana Jalil Ahsan Nadvi (written in Urdu). As regards the Hadiths, these are taken as such from the translations of well-known authorities, such as ``Sahih Muslim" by Abdul Hamid Siddique," Sahi-ul-Bukhari" Dr. Mohsin Khan, and "Mishkat" by Fazlul Karim. For tracing out some material facts regarding the brief background of the Islamic era at its nascent stage I had to consult The "Principles of Mohammedan Law" by Nosherwan H. Jhabwala, a well known figure in India. Besides, I have derived some material from the 'Musalman Khawind' written in Urdu by Mohammed Idris Ansari.

SABIRUDDIN, B.A. LL.B.

1

NIKAH (MARRIAGE)

The first step towards the constitution of a valid marriage is the initiation of a proposal (for marriage) from one party to the other. It may be in writing or otherwise. But it is absolutely necessary that it must be in unambiguous and cogent words, and must explicitly convey the intention of the sender. The acceptance of proposal by the wooed party finalises the matter, and results in the proclamation of *Nikah* by a Kadi or Moulvi on a fixed date. No writing of the *Nikah* proceedings is required. (Now-a-days, no doubt, the people have started to secure a Nikahnama signed by the parties duly attested by the witnesses as a proof of marriage, but it is not obligatory. Apperently, there is no harm in it). The only requisite is the presence of two male witnesses of sound mind, in whose presence the contract is effected. In case two males are not available, one male and two females can be made witnesses to the *Nikah*. A marriage without witnesses is irregular, but not void. (In Shia Law, however, witnesses are not required at all). It is also necessary that the proposal and the acceptance must be affected in the same meeting. A proposal made at one meeting and an acceptance made at another meeting do not constitute a valid marriage.

According to Muslim Law, marriage is a civil contract. Its object is to legalise sexual intercourse and the procreation of children. To constitute a valid marriage no formality or any religious ceremony is called for. The concept of a valid marriage (contract) requires that the parties must be of sound mind, and be otherwise competent to contract. The words "competent to contract" make it imperative that each party must have attained the age of puberity* and neither of them is debarred from making a contract. They must not be *lunatics or minors. In case of minor or lunatic the marriage can be contracted* by and through their guardians.. Such marriages can be ratified or rescinded afterwards by the parties if either of them so desires. According to Shia Law, the marriage of a minor or a lunatic arranged by a person other than father, or grand-father, is ineffective until it is ratified by the parties on attaining puberity.

It is also necessary that the consent of the parties must not have been obtained by force or fraud. A

According to the Hanafi school of thought puberity is presumed to have been attained on the completion of 15 years of age. Conversely in puberity begins with menstruation.

marriage celebrated under compulsion is invalid, but it can be legalised after ratification by the parties concerned.

Polyandry in Islam is strictly prohibited. Only Polygamy is allowed to the extent of having four wives at a time, and that too, under certain checks and restrictions.

Islam has prescribed certain categories of relations with whom marriage cannot be contracted on account of their consanguinity. No valid marriage can be contracted with one who is from own law. It cannot be contracted with paternal or maternal uncles and aunts. Similarly, no valid marriage can be contracted with wife's mother, or grand-mother, and wife's daughter or grand-daughter provided his own marriage is consummated. Marriage with foster brother or sister is also prohibited. No marriage can be contracted with father's wife. or son's wife, or any lineal descendants of them.

If a Sunni female marries outside her religion then that marriage is termed irregular, but not void. On the contrary, according to the Shia Law the parties to the marriage must be Muslims. If either of them is a non-Muslim, the marriage is unlawful. But a Sunni Muslim male may contract a valid marriage with a *Kitabia*,* or a fire-worshipper. A Muslim is forbidden from having

---

Kitabia as described by the *Shariah* is a *Jew* or *Christian*.

two wives at the same time who are real sisters. Similarly, marriage with a woman undergoing Iddat of her previous marriage is not valid. It is irregular.

Legally, after consummation of a valid marriage the husband becomes responsible for the payment of her dower. He is honour-bound to provide her maintenance, rights to enjoy the society, and upbringing of her infants. On the same footing, a wife also has to discharge certain corresponding duties towards her husband, such as to be faithful and obedient to him. Allowing him sexual intercourse, watching his interests at all costs, and suckling his children if he is not in a position to afford a wet-nurse.

2

IMPORTANCE OF A PIOUS WOMAN

> *Abdullah bin Omar reported Allah's messenger saying (Peace be on him and his progeny):*
>
> *"The whole world is a provision store, and the best object of benefit of the world is a pious woman".*
>
> (Sahih Muslim)

The words "best object of benefit of the world" in this *Hadith* are very vital, and meaningful. A pious woman is highly appreciated by the Holy Prophet (Peace be on him and his progeny). In Islam a pious woman is an asset not only for the family but also for the society. She will always bring happiness, trust and goodwill through her inherent amiable conduct and good behaviour. If she is sensible and a versatile " Momin " and able to distinguish the right from the wrong, the unlawful from the lawful, allowable from the prohibited (which is a must for a Muslim) there is no doubt, her family can enjoy life even in the face of worst calamities. Such a woman will always hold a family together and steer them through any sort of trouble. She will exhort the earning members of the family not to be attracted by bribery, ill-gotten or easily-gotton money. In every walk of life, she can achieve a prominent place for her and her family in the eyes of God and the world by surrendering her affairs to God's will.

A pious woman can herself say and compel others to say Namaz punctually in addition to other duties enjoined to them in accordance with the Divine Laws. Her patience, tolerance and perseverance can save the family from slipping into ignominy.

> *Abu Huraira (Allah be pleased with him) reported. Allah's Messenger (Peace be on him and his progeny) as saying:*
>
> *"A woman may be married for four reasons; for her property; for her high status; for her beauty and for her religious mindedness. So try to get one, who is religious-minded.*

(Muslim and Bukhari)

It is generally the worldly considerations, which predominate one's mind while making a choice for a woman to be contracted for marriage. The Holy Prophet (Peace be on him and his progeny) has always been exhorting his Noble Companions to make the religious piety of the woman to be the first choice. Following the actions of the Holy Prophet (Peace be on him and his progeny) and his noble companions, it is incumbent on us also to give preference to the last virtue of the woman, whom we intend to woo for marriage. It is a religious-minded wife only, who can discharge her duties honestly and sincerely towards her husband and society. We can skip the other minor defects of the lady if she has any. We come across many cases where beautiful girls generally are more interested in their beauty. Similarly a rich girl will feel superior to others.

*Restraining the **Ummah** from galloping after wealth the Holy Prophet (Peace be on him and his progeny) has said:*

"When you get a nice proposal from a righteous, religious - minded and God-fearing man for marriage, accept it, otherwise the earth shall loose its frustration, quarrels, disruption and plunder for you in retaliation.

(Tirmidhi)

At one other occasion the Holy Prophet said (Peace be on him and his progeny)

"If you reject a nice proposal and run after wealthy brides, (Note! that) a lot of your males will remain unmarried. This action of yours may give rise to various

crimes, the tragic end of the defiant
followers of Prophet Mosses is before
you."

During the days of the prophet-hood of Hadrath
Mosses the people used to seek wealthy spouses
and due to this rapacious fashion of the society, in
many good families girls grew old but not married till
their last breath. Tired of being a celibate some of
them used to elope with their paramours, if any, Imam
Malik, in the light of the Holy Qur'an, says that only the
virtue of being religious-minded in an expected spouse
must be sought for, and preferred. One should not
hanker after wealth. It may automatically knock at
one's door by the grace of God, He wishes so. A true
Muslim wife is the ideal wife who will always be
solicitious of other's welfare.

*Narrated Abu Huraira: Allah's Apostle
said :*

*"The best woman among the Camel
Riders, are the women of Quresh."
Another narrator said: The Prophet said,
(Peace be on him and his progeny)*

*"The righteous among the women of
Quresh are those, who are kind to their
younger ones, and who look after their
husband's property."*

(Sahih Bukhari)

The underlying idea that emerges from this Hadith is that a woman possessing the following two virtues are considered to be the best of all by the Holy Prophet (Peace be on him and his progeny)

(a)   In addition to her being religious-minded, she must possess the quality of being attentive and sensitive towards the welfare and good bringing up of the children; and

(b)   The quality of strictly protecting the wealth of her husband from being squandered up or going waste.

The Holy Prophet (Peace be on him and his progeny) said:

"The world is very alluring and enticing. God has sent us here with the object of testing us as to how we use it. So we must use it in the right way. Similarly, the woman is also a test for us, and therefore, we must use her also in the right and befitting way."

(Sahih Muslim)

The Holy Qur'an brings at par the wife and the husband by calling them a "Raiment for each other."

They are your garments and you are their garments"

(2.187)

Elucidating the words of the above verse Maulana

Abul A'la Maududi has stressed that the relation between husband and wife is like that between clothes and the body. Just as they are closed and fit into each other, and nothing intervenes between them, in the same way, husband and wife are closely related to each other and are source of natural comfort to each other.

The Holy Prophet (Peace be on him and his progeny) has said :

"The love and affection between a legally weded couple is such as is not thought of in any other bond of life. "

(Abu daud)

3

CHARACTER BUILDING

From time immemorial, oblivious of the consequences, man has been falling prey to his sexual desires even at the risk of his life, not to talk of honour, health, wealth and rectitude. Barring the *Apostles of Allah*, it seems, that certain degree of venality is an inherent part of human nature. The Apostle of Allah (Peace be on him and his progeny) has reiterated time and again to be vigilant and have strong grip over sexual passions as this is the biggest weakness. Even during the period of war of existence the enemies of Islam had thrown such baits to the faithfuls as a weapon against them, and history testifies that the bondsmen of Allah, by His grace, saved themselves from such tests in the past. They safely ignored such tests in the past. They safely ignored such enticements by not raising their eyes towards the scantily clad or totally naked girls enemy who had deputed them to divert the *faithfulls* from their mission.

It is a pity that today we do not emulate our

forefathers but let our passions run wild. This has resulted in many defeats and humiliations. May God save us from falling into ruin and lead us to do rightfully and legally what we do now illegally and immorally.

After the advent of Islam, humanity got a new dimension. The torch of monotheism illuminated the whole world. Worship of idols was given up. Immoral practices were stamped out. Conception of one - and only one God came in, Which was accepted. The people began to believe that God alone is the Creator, Nourisher, Sustainer, and the Dispenser of life after death.

They, irrespective of their caste, creed, or origin, learnt how to make the world a living paradise and a wave of character-building rose with ocean of Arabian desert in the garb of Qur'anic messages, which crossed even the Arabian boundaries within a very short period. The Arabs were transformed into a courageous, sacrificing, truth-loving strong & well organised nation. Thus they became the master of a new world where Qur'anic teachings were not forced upon people but were voluntarily accepted by all.

Dr. S.M.Iqbal, in his book "Realms of Peace" has described that a very well-known scholar of Vedanta, Swami Ram Tirath has rejected the theory that Islam was spread with the help of brute force or compulsion. He was of the view that Muslims defeated the Hindus because they were full of enthusiasm and faith (Vishwas). As a matter of fact, the Swami was very much influenced by the principles of Islam-particularly the idea of decentralization of wealth, and the theory of "giving" and "receiving". The Swami puts his arguments in this respect as under :-

> "According to Vedanta, the possession of any individual property is the most sacrilegious deed against one's Atma (Inner self). According to Vedanta, the only right the man has, is to give and not to take. If you have nothing to give, give up your body to be fed upon by worms. You are rich by what you give. Vedanta wants you to recognise the truth that all pleasure is in giving and not in asking or begging. Wherever you may in asking or begging. Wherever you may be, work in the position of a giver and never in the position of a begger, so that your work may be universal work and not personal in the least".

This is actually what the Qur'an says and the *Holy Prophet* (Peace be on him and his progeny) insists upon. He once said : "The upper hand (the hand that gives) is superior to, or better than the lower hand (the hand that receives)". Similarly, the theory of decentralization of wealth has its origin in Islam. Zakat (Obligatory alms) is a living example of this notion. Hard earned money is an exquisite diet for the Muslims. After migration to Madina from Mecca, the Muslims had nothing to live on. They were never taught begging, or getting any favour from the local inhabitants of Madina from Mecca, the Muslims had nothing to live on. They were never taught begging, or getting any favour from the local inhabitants of Madina for their personal benefit. There were taught to earn their livelihood by hard work. The prophet (Peace be on him and his progeny) preached not only social justice but also commanded to live a detached life, a life though not one of extreme penury, but of simplicity and contentment. In His view wealth or any avarice for its accumulation, is the greatest enemy of human. Once he had stated: "Had I been in my possession as much of the quantity of gold as is the size of the mountain Uhad, it would have added to my pleasure to give away the whole of it in the way of God, and there would not have passed more than three days when there would not have remained with me a dinar or dirham excepting an amount to liquidate a debit payable by me".

The Qur'an did not teach the faithfuls that they are really the owners or masters of wordly assets, and even life. It explicitly says: "God hath purchased of the believers their persons and their goods; for theirs (In return) is the garden (of Paradise). Then rejoice in the bargain which you have concluded: that is the achievement."

Sayed Abul A'la Maududi, expounding the Ayat (Verse) No. 131 of *Surah Albagrah* of the *Holy Qur'an.* has said : "Thus a Muslim is one, who surrenders himself completely to Allah and obeys him; who acknowledges Allah alone as his Lord, Master, Sovereign, Ruler, Law-giver, and God of worship, and who adopts the way of life prescribed by him." A tenacious belief that there is a Supreme Power, which is called God, and to whom man is answerable for his actions, is the crux of this conception. This conception gives rise to a sort of fear of God, which controls the man at every step. If there is no fear, it is possible that nobody may listen to anybody. The fear of God coupled with a strong sense of rectitude, and a desire for doing good to others motivates to distinguish evil from good.

In the light of the above definition it can be rightly said that the surrender to Allah has some specific conception. It behoves us to leave our all matters to God for His final decision. This deters the human from becoming wayward. In other words it is a fetter in his feet not to allow him to exceed his limits established by the Qur'an. A Muslim believes that God is All-powerful. He is omnipresent. He sees what a man does. or thinks. From womb to tomb he is enjoined to be within his limits as prescribed by the Qur'an.

The Holy Prophet said : (Peace be on him and his progeny). "God guarantees three kinds of man against His curse :-

1. One, who discharges his duties sincerely and faithfully towards God and his creation according to His commandments;

2. One, who solemnly not only determines to stick to his own wife/wifes only, but also refrains from every immoral act and does not see any other woman than his wife for his sexual urge; and

3. A crusader."

(Tirmidhi)

The words "sincerely" and "faithfully" are very meaningful in this *Hadith*. This conception requires a man to be selfless and devout beyond the reach of any personal desire. It is a matter of common knowledge that the various moods of a person are very rapidly changing. Life is always changing and that too rapidly. The human being as an individual is caught in its intricacies, which leads him to aberrations. The human being as a matter of fact, is the biggest mixture of opposites. Though he is weak, yet he claims to be strong enough to conquer the world. Though he is mortal, yet he accumulates wealth, constructs palaces, lives luxuriously as if he were an immortal. He is more sensitive than a bubble, but remains obdurate, and restless. Though he is made of clay, yet he becomes haughty and forgets God his creator. He forgets love for God, family, and humanity.

Some mystics are of the opinion that love can motivate a person to obey God, and the measure of its achievements is the service to humanity, dispensation of justice, dissemination of knowledge, helping the weak, easing the tension of the human mind. For this stupendous task of uplifting human society from the pitfalls and quagmires of sin and superstitions, greatest importance in Islam has been given to love and affection, which is sure to uproot the malaises. Man can win favour of God through his sincere love. The great saint *Baba Farid Masood Ganj-e-Shakar* has called the heart without love, a mere piece of flesh and nothing else.

The contents of the second part of *Hadith* are self-explantory. A person, who does not indulge in sexual immoralities, is certainly beyond the human level. It is thus patent that the *Hadith* in question is a warning to the humanity at large. Ibney Omar (Allah be pleased with him) reported Allah's Apostle as having said:

> *"None amongst you should outbid*

another in transaction, nor should he made proposal of marriage on the proposal made by someone else."

(Muslim & Bukhari)

This *Hadith* elucidates that we should be fair in all our transactions & dealings and be not a source of irritation, or agreement to others.

There are numerous instances where the girls were married to poor families and after marriage, by the grace of God, became rich. On the other hand there are girls who were married to well-to-do boys, but after marriage, had to live indignantly. The Holy Qur'an says that "God is All-Powerful." He can give wealth. He can take it back. What He does nobody knows."

If a person is really a "*Momin*" worldly wealth has no significance for him. God has sent a large number of Prophets to earth, of whom Prophet Mohammed (Peace be on him and his progeny) was the last. Besides, He has sent a large number of His friends (Aulias) also to earth, who purged the world of its inequities. If we study them, we will see that the longing for wealth and faith in God cannot co-exist in the heart of a man. Their wealth was their faith in Allah. They lived simply, shared others pangs and sorrows, did not eat at all for days together and fed others; remained bare-bodied, arranged clothes for the poor, remained exposed to inclement weather, but provided shelter to the needy masses; loved all indiscriminately; taught others how to shed pride, jealousy, hate, annoyance, back-biting, and other moral degradations. Fortunately, there is no dearth of such mystics amongst Muslims. They were thoroughly versed in the intellectual heritage of both esoteric and exoteric Islam. None of them preached abandonment of the world. What they gave up was not the world as such, but its attachment. They were of the opinion that the human should enjoy the world to the full, but should not fall a prey to its allurements, and should be in a position to run amuck to welcome the call of death as and when it reaches to him. *Hadrath Nizam Uddin Aulia*, a well known mystic, says that the human should not desert the world and inhabit the forests, but he should not desire to accumulate wealth depriving its legitimate and rightful owner i.e. the poor. *Hadarath Moin Uddin Chisti* (of Ajmer) once said : "Human should be bountiful like sun; generous and kind like ocean, and tolerant like earth." He too preached suppression of base desires. According to him, the object of one's life must be the service of humanity. Service to humanity is the service of God.

After attaining such a sublime place in life, human beings become Momin & Mutaqqi, about whom the mystics say, that whatever each a man does, it is Ibadat (Worship and devotion to God) Hadrath Sa'ad, a Companion of the Prophet (Peace be on him and his progeny) Once asked for his opinion; "Oh Allah's Apostle* should I give away my whole wealth to poor in charity?" The Prophet (Peace be on him and his progeny) replied: "keeping in view the object of pleasing God, whatever a man does, it tantamounts to "Ibadat", so much so a morsel of food offered to his wife is also 'Ibadat'.

In family life it is true that the benedictions of Nikah create exemplary love between husband and wife. The proof of the sincerity of love between the husband and the wife is automatically adduced if the beloved prefers to share the vicissitudes of life smilingly with her lover. The sincerity between them impresses upon them that they must tolerate the pangs howsoever unbearable they may be: face every misfortune befallen on them manfully, and not to desert each other, even if he or she is a beggar. A fortunate woman lives with her husband happily and enjoys life with him. Various instances are there to

---

Words 'Ibadat' postulates three ingredients
(1)   worship and devotion to the Almighty;
(ii)   submission and obedience to the Almighty;
(iii) subjugation and service to the Almighty.
The words Muttaqi and Momin are synonymous to each other in meaning. Syed Abu A'la Maududi, in his "Meaning of the Qur'an has defined that Muttaqi is one, who fears Allah; discriminates between good and evil, and intends to be righteous, and truth-loving. Abdullah Yusuf Ali in his "The glorious Qur'an" has gone a little farther while giving the following three pre-requisites of a Muttaqi: (i) The fear of God (which is the beginning of the wisdom); (ii) Restraint, or guarding one's tongue, hand, and heart from evil; and (iii) hence righteousness, piety and good conduct.

prove that poor but religious-minded husbands shower more love upon their wives in comparison to wealthy ones, who seldom have, or have no time what so ever to take care of their wives, not to talk of loving them. The Holy Qur'an says that one must bank upon his own strength of arms for earning the wealth instead of seeking to get it from others.

> The Holy Prophet said : (Peace be on him and his progeny).
> "Even a tinge of pride in a man disqualifies him from entering into Paradise."

Listening to it some companion enquired: "Oh Allah's Prophet. Is the wearing of decent clothes and good shoes etc. synonymous to pride"? The Prophet (Peace be on him and his progeny) replied: " No It is not pride. God is sublime and likes subtilities. Pride constitutes arrogance, egoism, and defiance of God's laws and looking down upon the bondsman of Allah."

The Holy Qur'an in Surah 'A'raaf, section 2, Ayat No. 11, 12 and 13 has said as under :

> 11.   It is We Who created you
>   And gave you shape;
>   Then We bade the Angels
>   Bowed down to Adam & they Bowed
>   down; not so Iblis;
>   He refused to be of those
>   Who bow down.

12.   (God) Said: "What prevented
       Thee from bowing down
       When I commanded thee ?
       He Said : Thou didst create
       Me from fire, and him from clay."

13.   (God) Said : "Get thee down
       From this : it is not
       For thee to be arrogant
       Here : get out, for thou Art of the
       meanest (of creation)

These dialogues between *Iblis* and *Allah* amply clarify that the egoism and arrogance of *Iblis* turned him out of the Heavens. If the *Iblis*, once a venerable angel of Allah, can be punished on account of his pride can we be spared in the court of Allah for identical offence ?

Abdullah Bin A'mir reported that the Holy Prophet (Peace be on him and his progeny) one day in my house, when my mother called me and said : "Come! I will give you something." The Prophet (Peace be on him and his progeny) enquired from her. "What will you give him?" "Palm" My mother replied. The Holy Prophet (Peace be on him and his progeny) said; " If you have not given him anything, you would have committed a sin (of telling a lie)

(Abu Daud)

Abdullah Bin Masood said; *"Telling a lie is not allowable-either in joke or otherwise. It is also not allowable not to fulfil the promises made with children".*

(Al-Adab-ul-Maruful Bukhari)

These *Hadiths* tell us that we should not tell a lie at all.

4

EXTRAVAGANCE IN MARRIAGE

The Holy Prophet has said (Peace be on him and his progeny)

"The Nikah not monetarily taxing (in nature) the parties and not creating unwanted fuss for the intermediaries and the participants in any way, is the most benedictory one."

(Al Behaqi)

In our present society people spare no effort in selecting a well-to-do family for their children. They treat the marriages of their children as a means of siphoning other's wealth into their own coffers. On the other hand, the wooed party too takes much pride in lavishly spending the money in such marriages only for the sake of his ego. So much so, it is generally seen that many guardians or parents become pauper after incurring back-breaking expenses of marriages, particularly of their daughters. Either they raise heavy and crippling loans or sell their leftovers to meet such profligate expenses and roam about like vanquished soldiers thereafter. They do not realise as to what extent their hypocrisy has eaten into the future of their own children, and fail to assess the precise magnitude of the extravagance at the proper time. Extravagant marriages badly fell upon their already tottering economic conditions and married couple do not have harmony. Such marriages are bad for the society as a whole, as the children have to suffer for it through-out their life. It is, therefore, in the light of this Hadith, not only advisable, but imperative that we should refrain from such extravagance. The uncalled for pomp and show, in order to gain transient applause and false praises, is against the tenets of Islam. We must control these expenses so that our children can be on sound footing in the future. One redeeming feature is that today Governments are passing laws to restrict extravagance and pomp in marriage.

5

A VIRTUOUS WIFE

The status of woman before the advent of Islam was absolutely different. The Holy Qur'an *whenever says "Ya Aiyyohan Nas "Ya Aiyyohal Lazi"* it accosts equally man and woman both. Its directions are for both. In Europe, even today, a woman cannot identify herself through her individual name. Till her marriage, she is called Miss Thomas, and immediately after marriage she becomes Mrs. Jones. She loses her own individuality. Such inferiority in the status of woman was never thought of in Islam. Whether she is called Fatma or Aisha, she is always Fatma or Aisha.

It is only the benedictions of the Qur'anic laws alone, that after the death of Caliph Othoman, when an internal strife among the Muslims simmered, a militant section of the Muslims gathered under the banner of *Hadrath Aisha.* It was quite a new idea for the masses that a frail lady could be their leader, but they did so because the Holy Qur'an had unambiguously declared the status of woman. It is thus evident that the Muslims of that century knew that woman had an equal status with man according to Divine Laws. There are numerous instances when the ladies, after proclamation of the Islamic laws, were encouraged to show and prove their real existence, latent talents, and tremendous capacity to work in every field. It is impossible to mention all of them here.

This actually negates what critics of Islam contend that the status of woman in Islam is inferior to that of man. Islam, no doubt has one restriction imposed on them for ever, and that is that they are not allowed to be unabashed, unchaste or unfaithful. Every field of work is open to them, but there is no place for degradation or immorality.

Abu Omamah reported from, the Messenger of Allah, as saying :

> *"Next to fear of Allah, the believers find nothing good for them than virtuous wives. If (the husband) bids her, she obeys him; if he looks at her, she gives him pleasure; if she gives him a promise she fulfills it; and if he absents from her, she guards herself and his property."*

(Nasai)

This Hadith is self-explanatory. A good wife can live with her poor husband happily. The best house is that where infallible sincerity resides. The exemplary house is that where the wife looks after the property of the husband, and spends the money with due care, so that no room is left for any wastage. Good qualities in a sensible wife lead the husband to the gates of paradise in this very world. Unfortunately, the youths of today have a penchant for such glamorous wives who have a natural aptitude for singing and dancing in parties, and in displaying their physical assets. They feel pride in moving about in tight trousers inviting the onlookers. Can we, in the light of the above *Hadith*, say that we are true followers of the Prophet? (Peace be on him and his progeny).

I am not against freedom for women. Their role in society must be bolstered. Rights of the husbands and the wives have been apportioned fairly and equitably in the Qur'an itself. But there is no room for moral turpitude in Islam. Presently all the evils of the world can be seen in our society, as if these have been injected into us. The so-called advanced society does not give us shelter from the curses of Allah, but pushes us towards Hell instead. Still, it is time for us to submit to God and offer our sincere and unconditional contrition, for the flagrant violation of *His Laws*. Our endeavour to achieve mundane gains only is very mean and perverse. If we do not turn towards our original faithful ways, we would be ruined. Crying over the past or even glorifying it cannot throw in our laps any material gain, What we were yesterday, nobody is concerned with.

Jabir reported that Allah's Messenger (Peace be on him and his progeny) once saw a woman. He came to his wife Zainab, and made love to her. He then went to his Companions and told them.

> "The woman advances and returns in the shape of Devil, and when any one of you see a woman, and feel fascination towards her, go to your wife, for, that will repel what you feel in your heart."

(Muslim)

The Messenger of Allah (Peace be on him and his progeny) instructed people by setting an example himself. He observed the incident from the point of view of a common man, and not of a "Companion, or a Wali".

He simply saw a woman without being affected in the least by her. He himself was chaste and pious to the marrow of his bones, and had perfect control over himself, so the idea of any evil could in no way cross his mind, but since this cannot be the case with an ordinary human being, he, in order to give them practical guidance, in the matter of the promptings of sex, told them to go to their wives under such conditions, as sexual repression is no remedy for it. Sexual instinct is an innate impulse of man and it should be satisfied by legitimate means rather than repressing it. The very sight of a woman, who appears to be a nymph causes a flutter in his mind and heart. If he goes beyond the limits, and gives a practical shape to his '*seeing*' he degrades himself in the eyes of the Creator, and the world, and particularly in the eyes of his wife, despite the fact that he keeps her ignorant of his deeds. But whenever he gets some time to think about such acts, he is sure to feel ashamed in his sub-conscience, if not openly before his wife, whose right he has deliberately snatched from her and showered it over another woman for momentary pleasure.

The sentence "*Woman advances and returns in the shape of Devil*" should not be misconstrued to mean that Islam regards the woman as a Devil. What it means is that when a glance at a woman arouses some sexual sensation in the onlooker, or he is so much infatuated and charmed by the looks of a woman that even her thought incites his baser desire, he should adopt the right course to go to his wife and satisfy himself instead of repressing his desire or fulfilling it from somewhere else. Conversely, if he does not do so, it is evident that the Devil will mislead him, and he is bound to commit some crime. The Holy Qur'an has appreciated the people, who keep their eyes down cast. The command of God is to stick to one's own wife only, otherwise the Satan may lead the wife also away. She may also imitate her husband after knowing about his misdeeds and finding herself unable to prevent him from such acts in future she may also be attracted towards a man of her own choice. God protect us from such satanic attitude in life. The Holy Prophet said (Peace be on him and his progeny)

> "Don't cast an eye on a (stranger) woman second time. If it is cast all of a sudden, and unintentionally, only once, there is no harm. In re-seeing her our desire comes in, which negatives the theory of self-restraint."

> (Abu Daud, Tirmidhi & Dami)

The prophet (Peace be on him and his progeny) addressed this Hadith to Hadrath Ali direct, perhaps due to the reason that He knew it well that the latter would be a nucleus of *Aulias* (Allah's friends) who will preferably give practical shape to the principles of Islam more commendably. This *Hadith* is a lesson for those fake *Pirs* (Mystics), who allow unhesitatingly the unknown woman to enter their periphery, and take personal services from them. Are they better than Hadrath Ali, who is prevented from seeing other woman a second time ? Such Pirs have forgotten that the Holy Prophet (Peace be on him and his progeny) on another occassion has remarked: "I don't shake hand with a stranger woman." It is obvious that he was not in favour of even touching his hand with that of some other woman.

Now come to the customs prevalent in the so-called advanced society of today, where we take pride in intermixing with other woman freely, sometimes on the plea of our advancement and changing norms of society and sometime on thinking that there is no harm in it and say : "We have no bad intention for any of them." On various occasion it has been seen that the crooked men, while mixing with the other women, try to touch them and feign that they have not done anything wrong. Mixing with the ladies in the society is now-a-days considered to be the symbol of elevation of one's standard of life, and proof of his upgradation of moral virtues. Such persons are considered to be men of etiquates, and commendable manners. The more one is cheeky and obdurate, the more civilized he is branded, despite the fact the woman-folks are generally subjected to catcalls, vulgar remarks and wolfish stare from the same civilized elements of society. As a matter of fact society is trying to erase the distinction between the male and the female. We generally come across lot of such incidents in our daily life, where the boisterous persons unintentionally slaughter the morality in order to reform it, but they do not know that their efforts to reshape the society in this way are baseless. What is required to bring changes in society is not known to them. The present measures to improve the norms of society are very deceptive and certainly are not the sign of health but symptoms of disease. Instead of advancing, the society is relegating back into the stone age perhaps, where the people lived naked, and did whatever they liked. The difference between the norms of today and of that age is that the first mentioned are not totally naked. They certainly do what the stone agers used to do, but indifferent garb. Only the cloak is changed. It is a pity that we are caught in the snare laid by the Satan despite the forewarning of our Holy Prophet (Peace be on him and his progeny). Such persons are hypocrites. They lack sincerity and righteousness, and are motivated by prejudices. It can also be said beyond doubt that they do not like to see the world progressing & thriving in the real shape.

Narrated Uqaba bin A'mir: Allah's Apostle! Said:

"Beware of entering upon the ladies."

A man from the Ansars said : Allah's Apostle! what about Al-hemu (The inlaws of the wife) The Prophet replied: (Peace be on him and his progeny) "The in-laws of the wife are death themselves."

(Tirmidhi)

On another occasion one of the companions enquired :

"O Apostle of Allah ! can *Satan* misguide you also ? "The Holy Prophet replied (Peace be on him and his progeny)

"Yes! He tries so, but God has endowed
me tremendous power to overcome him.
He can do no harm to me".

In the light of the above *Hadith* the question
arises; Can Satan spare a common man, particularly
the youths, who are full of vigour and vitality, from
being enticed towards the stranger woman, when he
endeavours to attack even the Holy Prophet (Peace
be on him and his progeny). Are we stronger than the
Holy Prophet (Peace be on him and his progeny) in
resisting the temptations offered by Satan ? The
Prophet (Peace be on him and his progeny) once said
that women are the net of Satan. He entraps men
through them. Is there any further need of elaboration
on this issue ? God may save us from *His wrath* and
protect us from the cunningness of Satan.

Jabir reported that the Messenger of
Allah said: (Peace be on him and his
progeny)

"When one of you see a woman for
marriage and then, if you are able to
have a look at her whom you wish to
marry, let you do it."

The scholars of the Islamic jurisprudence have
consensus of opinion that a girl may be seen before
marriage as the future of the husband and the wife
depends on the better choice of each other. If the girl

is of the husband's choice, there are chances of his being subdued to her beauty, or any other quality, and he may not run about greedily, and the very object of Nikah is to keep both the spouses exclusively for each other. *Hadrath Mugharib-Bin-Sha'aba* has referred to an incident of his own marriage when the Holy Prophet (Peace be on him and his progeny) enquired from him if he had seen the girl with whom he would be having abiding binding and covenant. The Holy Prophet (Peace be on him and his progeny) made it further clear that the eternal love between the two depends upon having a bride of one's own choice, and vise versa, and their future as well as of their generation becomes secured from being ruined due to the incogenial atmosphere of the house, irrespective of their financial status. Atleast the domestic life may be freed from mutual recrimination if of both live affectionately.

> The Prophet (Peace be on him and his progeny) said:

> "Reprobate are the males, who see greedily towards the other women. Similarly, reprobate are the women, who see the other men rapaciously."

The significance of this *Hadith* is pretty clear. I have discussed in the earlier lines the repercussions of our carelessness in the matter of proximity of men with another woman. Satan may lay trap for anybody. Hafiz Ibne Qayam has analysed this theory in a few lines as under :-

> "A rapacious look of a man of an unknown woman sows seed of sin in the soil of his heart, in which the plant of sexual urge germinates. The Plant thrives through the further soft corner and longing for sinful and amorous acts in one's heart. The tentacles of immorality, like the twigs of the plant thereafter sprout from furthering and strengthening the evil intention, which in fact, bear fruit in the shape of commission of a sexual sin".

Seeing a blind male the veiled ladies generally think that he is not seeing them and so there is no harm if the latter see him. They think that the philosophy of wearing veils is one sided and that is that no male should see the female. It is a very wrong notion. No doubt a blind man is not able to see a woman, but she does see him. Some lustful intent may grab her. The philosophy of wearing a veil before others is that neither party should see each other, except those, who are not in the prohibited degree of relationship.

6

THRUSTING OF DECISION ON ADULT GIRLS

Hadrath Ibne Abbas said that a sui juris girl once approached the Holy Prophet (Peace be on him and his progeny) and said : "O Apostle of Allah ! My parents have married me with a youth of not my choice: What should I do?" The Holy Prophet (Peace be on him and his progeny) replied: "You are not minor, you are at full liberty either to rescind the nikah or maintain it."

(Abu Daud)

The Marriage of an adolescent girl forcibly with somebody not of her liking is prohibited in the eye of the Holy Prophet (Peace be on him and his progeny). On the other hand, if the girl shuns to be called a divorcee after rescinding the marriage, she should remember that God is always with steadfasts, people and his tremendous power either to convert her spite into affection for her husband, or devise some other means for her.

RESPONSIBILITY OF PARENTS

Abu Sayeed and Ibne Abbas reported that the Messenger of Allah said :

"Whosoever has got a son born unto him, give him a good name and good manners. When he attains maturity, get him married. If he attains maturity and the parents do not get him married, and then the son commits a sin, his sin will fall upon his parents."

(Albehaqi)

It is thus the duty of the parents to arrange suitable match for their children according to the laws of Islam. The carelessness of the parents may spoil the health, wealth and character of their dear sons.

The Holy Prophet (Peace be on him and his progeny) said :

"If a girl exceeding 12 years of age, is not married and a sin is committed by her, her parents shall be held for it."

(Albe)

How thought-provoking this Hadith is in its character, can be seen. It is a warning to those careless parents who inspite of witnessing untoward happenings everyday, are oblivious of their daughter's welfare. A girl is an open invitation to evils.

Even the slightest slip on her part can degenerate the whole society. If the girl is of age, she must be married even without dowry, if it is not available., Hadrath Fatma, the noble daughter of the Holy Prophet (Peace be on him and his progeny) was married without dowry. She was given a handmill to grind corn for the family in dowry. Our daughters have no excellence over the noble daughter of the Holy Prophet (Peace be on him and his progeny).

7

SONG SINGING IN MARRIAGES.

Hadrath Aisha (Allah be pleased with her) reported:

"Allah's Apostle (Peace be on him and his progeny) contracted marriage with me in the month of Shawwal and took me to his house as bride during Shawwal, and (note!) among the wives of Allah's Messenger (Peace be on him and his progeny) no wife was dearer to Him as I."

Hadrath Aisha liked the women (of her family particularly) should enter their houses as bride during the month of Shawwal. This even explicitly condemns the superstitious way of thinking of those, who consider certain dates, days, and months to be inauspicious for celebrating marriages. Generally the month of Shawwal is taken to be unpropitious by the ladies, but this is wrong. Conversely, as is evident from the above *Hadith* marriage in the month of Shawwal is a source of blessing and benedictions, as this is one among the *Sunnahs*. In order to erase the very cause of such vague and baseless ideas, the Holy Prophet (Peace be on him and his progeny) has deliberately celebrated His marriage in the month of Shawwal.

> Narrated Ar-Rabbi, the daughter of Muawwidth Bin Afra :
>
> "After the consummation of my marriage, the Holy Prophet (Peace be on him and his progeny) came to me and sat on my bed as far from me as you are sitting now, and our little girls started beating the tambourines and reciting elegic verses mourning my father, who had been killed in the battle of Badr. One of them said: 'Among us is a Prophet, who knows what will happen tomorrow''. On that, the Holy Prophet (Peace be on him and his progeny) forbade the girls to say so, because none knows (Except Allah) the future."
>
> This Hadith highlights three important things :-

1.   The verses not containing exaggeration or lie may be read or sung.:

2.   Such songs may be sung on such occasions only; and

3.   Nobody knows the future except *Allah*

Allama Akmal Uddin is of the opinion that the beating of *Daff* and singing songs by the relatives of the bridgeroom and the bride on the occasion of Nikah is also allowable. Similarly, such singing on the occasion of Id, circumcision, and other occasions is equally allowable.

> Hadrath Aisha has said : "I Happened to attend a marriage party at the residence of Ansar. The ceremonies were absolutely simple and unsophisticated. Seeing such simplicity, the Prophet (Peace be on him and his progeny) said to the Host: `You have no duff players with you as you are Ansar, who are very fond of singing songs on such occasions."

(Bukhari)

Hadrath Aisha has said that there was Ansar girl in her house (Aisha's house) whose marriage she celebrated very simply. The Prophet, (Peace be on him and his progeny) asked her if she had arranged any singing on that occasion as the Ansars are very fond of it.

The songs in those days were not sung with the help of Harmoniums., or instruments, but with the help of *Duff* only, Songs consisting of good verses, coupled with the duff-beating were permissible in those days and are still today.

Amir Bin Sa'd said that once he had occasion to take part in a marriage party at the house of a companion of the Holy Prophet (Peace be on him and his progeny) where a programme of singing was on. The house wives and the girls of the neighbourers were singing. On my admonishing the householder I was told that the programme is allowable by the Apostle of Allah (Peace be on him and his progeny) on such occassions.

Such marriages are really appreciable. No pomp and show; no dowry; no drum-playing; no dazzling lights. In order to overawe the others we have invented so many formalities to be observed in marriages, which are absolutely superfluous, and have no place in our social system *Hadrath Adam Nadauri* has demanded us to renounce such uncalled for traditions being observed in our society. He is of the opinion that the children born of such marriage are illegitimate.

VENUE OF NIKAH

The Prophet (Peace be on him and his progeny) said:

"Promulgate the Nikah with duff-beatings. It is better to hold it in a mosque so that everybody present there for saying prayer, witnesses it."

(Tirmidhi)

The performance of Nikah on Friday, after noon prayer, is, therefore, a sign of benedictions. It is also a *Sunnah*. The Holy Prophet (Peace be on him and his progeny) held the Nikah of his dearest daughter Fatma with Hadrath Ali in mosque.

8

RIGHTS & DUTIES INTERSE

> The Holy Prophet (Peace be on him and his progeny) said :
>
> "Pay her dower; provide her all facilities and treat her affectionately and humanly."

This *Hadith* is self-explanatory. Payment of dower to the wife, accordingly, is obligatory (Dower is separate chapter). So far as the 'Providing of facilities to the wife and 'treat her affectionately and humanly' are concerned, there are innumerable Hadiths and Quranic injuctions on this subject. The husband, who misbehaves with his wife, does not pay her due regard, falls out with her on trifles, and castigates her not in commensuration with her fault, is not considered to be a good husband by the Holy Prophet (Peace be on him and his progeny). If he thrusts his own will upon her arbitrarily or despotically, he commits a sin incompatible with the principles of this *Hadith*.

The *Holy Qur'an*, in *Surah Al-Nisa*, Ayat No. 33.34

has abundantly cleared the status of the husband vis-a-vis his wife.

> "Men are the managers of the affairs of the women because Allah has made them superior and because men spends his wealth on woman. Virtuous women are, therefore, obedient. They guard their rights carefully in their absence under the care of Allah. As for those woman whose defiance you have cause to fear, admonish them and keep them apart from your beds and beat them. Then, if they submit to you, do not look for excuses to punish them: note it well that there is Allah above you, Who is Supreme and Great."

On another occasion in *Surah Baqr*, Ayat No. 228, the Holy Qur'an has equalised the husband and the wife in status in regard to their right inter se.

> "Wives have the same rights as the husbands have on them in accordance with the generally known principles. Of course, men are a degree above them in status and above all is Allah, the Almighty, the All powerful, and All-wise."

This Ayat has established the upperhand of the husband again. In Section 28 Ayat No. 228, The Holy Qur'an has stressed emphatically that the wife has an

equal status with man, but the husband has some
superiority over her.

> "And women shall have rights similar to
> the rights against them, according to
> what is equitable; but men have a degree
> (of advantage) over them. And God is
> exalted in power."

In the light of the above, it is absurd to presume
that the wife has any inferior status in comparison to
the husband. But due to her being of a weaker sex,
she has been advised to seek protection of her
husband so far as the wordly affairs are concerned.
The husband, no doubt, has more power: more
strength; more alacrity; more maturity than the wife.
As a matter of fact in the realm of household affairs the
husband possesses a position of a King, but not of an
absolute monarch, whereas the wife of a Prime
Minister's. The first, no doubt, wields veto power and
the latter has to yield to his decisions quietly and
patiently. In the houses where the position is reverse,
it is seen that the house is not a sweet home, but a
bitter one. On the other hand the king too should give
due regard to the susceptibilities of the Prime Minister,
and should not get his orders implemented and
obeyed despotically. If he wants to make his home a
real good home, he must take the wife into his
confidence while making decisions.

Mr. Nisar Ahmad, in his book "The Fundamental teachings of Qur'an and Hadiths", has tried to pin point certain rights and duties between the husband and the wife in these words :

"Islam lays down in express and definite terms the rights and duties which spring from marriage. Before Islam, especially the wife had no locus standi either in law or in society. The Qur'an and the Holy Prophet effected a complete revolution in the status and position of women. Now instead and position of women. Now instead of 'gate of evil' 'the road to inequity' the poison of asp', she became a safeguard for her husband against sin, a bulwark against inroads of the evil, a lighthouse of virtue that saves the man from destruction, and a great force with potential to transform male rudeness into angelic nobility. The mutual relations of husband and wife and their respective duties, as directed by the Holy Qur'an and Hadith, may be summarised as under :

(A) Duties of husband towards wife :-

　　　1. She is a trust in his hand. He shall treat her kindly.

　　　2. He shall not be too strict to her in order to make her conform to his views.

　　　3. He shall not hate her.

　　　4. A mild beating (with tooth-stick etc. not

with whip or stick) admonition, or separation from bed, is allowed only in some extreme cases.

5. He shall give enough time to keep company with his wife in amusing pursuits.

6. He shall allow none to interfere in their conjugal matters and pry into the secrets of their sexual life.

7. Besides providing food and clothing, he should spend sometime for his wife.

8. In case of several wives, distribution of companionship with each wife shall be made equally.

9. He shall provide food, clothing, and abode to her.

10. in case of death, the wife gets a share in husband's property and the husband in wife's property.

11. He shall give her education (especially about the fundamentals of Islam).

(B) Duties of wife towards husband

1. The wife is bound to live with her husband unless she is unfit for conjugal relations and shall not, deny him pleasure of flesh.

2.   She shall be obedient in all respect and administer his comforts by shortening her religious duties.
3.   She shall not spend out of the property of her husband without permission.
4.   She shall guard her chastity.
5.   She shall look after his possessions in his absence and shall protect herself against sins."

The Holy Prophet (Peace be on him and his progeny) was very reluctant to allow beating of woman as a last resort. He further advised not to beat atleast on face, or so severely as to inflict any physical marks on her body. If a mere light admonition proves effective, there is no need to resort to a severe step.

The above writer has very rightly observed "In short, husband and wife both are equal partners in life having quite distinct functions, which are suited to his or her nature. The husband is mainly required to earn for the maintenance of the family, and the wife is responsible for the management of the household and the bringing up of the children."

A common cause of squabbles between a husband and a wife is often the presence of some relatives in the house, such as parents, brothers sisters of the husband and so on. The husband and wife, sometimes do not get enough liberty to enjoy their married life to the full. The husband continues to tolerate their presence due to his consanguinity, or otherwise. He fears them that they will call him a hen-pecked husband, if he ever tries to alienate them. But the wife, a new-comer, from her own kith and kins, feels irritated at their frequent interventation in matters pertaining to their private life. Such situation is not good. On such occasion, the parents especially and others in common, instead of extinguishing the fire, stoke the flames sometimes by favouring the husband and sometimes the wife. The seed of discord and misunderstanding is thus sowed between them, which after sometimes, is bound to bear fruit in the shape of fighting - perhaps unending; sometimes culminating into divorce. This is the irony of fate that the persons responsible for such occurrances never mend their ways, and rather incite the combatants.

The wife under such circumstances wants to live separately from the inlaws and the husband desists from yielding to her desire.

As a matter of fact, we must not force her to live with our parents if she desires otherwise, and if we forsee that no justice will be done to her. In Islam the principle of *Justice and equity* in such matter has to prevail. It is seen that even some educated youths fall a prey to such malaise. This is not good. One must be fair, temperate, and even-handed with the wife vis-a-vis others. The parents also have certain and definite place for them. Neither party should be subjected to uncalled for prejudice and excesses.

A very peculiar situation arises when a person has a limited sources of earning, and is not able to feed his parents. He should give first preference to his own domestic expenses. The parents themselves should realise the depleted economic condition of their sons (if it is so) and should not create unwarranted tension for their sons by demanding money from them from time to time, or insist on some fixed amount for them payable after certain intervals. It is often seen that a man fails to do justice with both the parties simultaneously due to his limited means. Unfortunately, both the parties pull their legs, and the poor sons occasionally are confronted with difficulties. For such persons, the Holy Qur'an has very clearly expressed that the rights of the wife have priority over others'. Maulana Ashraf Ali Thanvi, in his book 'Bahishti Zever' has noted that the husband should give first priority to the rights of his wife, so far as the proportion of the obligatory duties are concerned. The wife has every right to insist on her husband to live separately from the in-laws (her inlaws) if financial resources are limited, and the husband should not prevail upon her to live with his parents.

Every daughter-in-law alongwith her husband,

has a right to think about her future in the light of financial and social conditions prevailing under certain circumstances of the family. She is at liberty to devise ways and means of saving something for the rainy days for their family from out of the meagre earnings of her husband provided she is sensible. Her in-laws may not be getting their financial expectation fulfilled, but they should have patience and feel happy with their lot, which they get from their married sons.

The Holy Qur'an in *Surah Al-Nisa*, has stressed upon the husbands.

> "Give the women (on marriage) their dower as a free gift; but if they, of their own good pleasure remit any part of it to you, take it and enjoy it with cheers."

On another occassion the Holy Qur'an has provided :

> "Men are the protector and maintainer of women because God has given them more strength than the wife, and because they support them from their means. Therefore, the righteous women are devotedly obedient, and guard in husband's absence what God would have them guarded."

Similarly, the Holy Qur'an has further commanded:

"Lodge them where you live according to your means, and injure them not to straighten them, And if, they are pregnant, spend on them, until they lay down their burden."

On the same footing, admonishing and reminding the wife of her obligatory duty towards her husband a *Hadith* says :-

"Whenever a man calls his wife to his bed, and she refuses, and then he passes the night in angry mood; the angels curse her till she gets up at dawn,"

According to some other report (quoted by Bukhari and Muslim) the Holy Prophet (Peace be on him and his progeny) has said :

"By Him in whose hand there stands my life, if a man calls his wife to his bed, and she turns away from him, He, who is in the Heaven is displeased with her, till she pleases her husband."

Bukhari & Muslim

Abu Huraira reported that the Messenger of Allah (Peace be on him and his progeny) said :

"Had I enjoined to make prostration to anybody, I would have enjoined a woman to prostrate before her husband."

(Tirmidhi)

Reminding the ladies of their duties, the Holy Prophet (Peace be on him and his progeny) and the Holy Qur'an have reiterated the importance of the depth of the relations between them. The Holy Qur'an protects the ladies from tyrannical attitude of men but also empowers the man to set the wife right wherever necessary, but in the light of injuctions of the Shariah:

> "As to those women on whose part you fear disloyalty and ill-conduct, admonish them (first), (next) refuse to share their beds, and (last) beat them lightly; but if they return to obedience, see not against them means of (annoyance)."

It is also seen that some of the mothers-in-law (of the ladies) are very mischievous in nature. They create trouble for the sons and daughters-in-law out of their ignorance of the *Divine Laws*, or lack of common sense, though sometimes inadvertantly, and in good faith. They poison their son's ears against the daughters-in-law and cause disputes between them. Perhaps these happenings occur in every house, irrespective of its financial status. This is somewhat impertinent on the part of the relatives whether they are mothers-in-law or sisters-in-law. They must think that the new girl has also every right of participating in family matters after her marriage. The mother-in-law forgets that once she too was somebody's daughter-in-law. They take the daughter-in-law as an intruder, or alien, Unless such tendencies are removed, ill will and disharmony will continue to prevail. Being the senior member of the family, it is the duty of the mother-in-law not to create circumstances for their children who may find themselves cornered, The result of such actions can ruin their own kith and kins for ever. Such mothers-in-law shall be put to task in the court of Allah on the day of *resurrection, where nobody will avail of anybody else.*

It will be an in-justice, if I forget to advert to the duties of the married sons towards their aged and physically weak parents. Owing to their growing age their temperament generally becomes childish. Sometimes they may suffer from some illness and have nothing with them to depend on. As they are weak and feeble they need others support. All the avenues of earnings are shut to them. Their only hopes are their sons. Whatever meagre they had saved during their lifetime, had been spent either on the education of their children, or on the latter's marriages. They look towards their sons for their upkeep and welfare and think that their sons are not aware of their need, their long cherished desires of 'having good sons' fall flat,. This matters them, feel lonely in the world and their patience gives way. They have nothing to do except ruminating over their past. It is granted that both married sons and parents face this sort of problems. The sons should therefore take care of their parents. Daughters-in-laws should also be liberal to them and should treat them as their own parents. Due regard must be given to them. The children are after all young and have capacity and courage to combat difficulties, There are several Quranic injuctions and *Hadiths* in this respect to guide us. In *Surah Luqman, Section 2 (Ruku two) Ayat No. 14,* the Holy Qur'an has pronounced :

> "And we have enjoined on man
> (To be good) to his parents:
> In travail upon travail
> Did his mother bear him,
> And in years twain
> Was his weaning (Here
> The Command), "Show gratitude
> To me and to thy parent:
> To me is (thy final) Goal."

Besides, the following *Hadith* has elucidated:

> Abu Huraira report; that the Apostle of Allah (Peace be on him and his progeny) has said :

> "He be accursed." (He repeated this sentence thrice) Some noble Companions enquired:" About whom Oh Allah's Prophet (Peace be on him

and his progeny) did you utter so ?" The Holy Prophet (Peace be on him and his progeny) replied: "About him, who found his mother, or father, or both in senility, and did not enter Paradise through serving them."

Maulana Jalil Ahsan Nadvi, in his book *Safine-e-Nijat'* has narrated a very remarkable story, which is the best on this subject, and must be remembered by every Muslim.

"At the time of death a youth could not utter the *Kalima Tayyaba (La Ilaha El-Lal-Lah,, Mohammadur-Rasul Allah)* by his tongue. His attendance were perplexed and dazed. The matter was referred to the Holy Prophet (Peace be on him and his progeny), who came to him and enquired if his parents were alive. It was revealed that his mother was alive. The Holy Prophet (Peace be on him and his progeny) who came to him and enquired.

"How your son treats you,? The mother replied: He is a good boy, but after marriage, he has ceased to look after me, and I have to do labour work earning my both ends meet'. I am annoyed with him."

The Holy Prophet (Peace be on him and his progeny) suggested the lady to pardon her son. The mother replied 'No'. He has teased me a lot I cannot pardon him.' The Prophet (Peace be on him and his progeny) ordered the attendants to prepare a huge fire for his alive-burning. The mother moved a little and implored: 'How can I see my son burning alive.' The prophet (Peace be on him and his progeny) replied: 'He shall be burnt in the Hell for ever'. The mother took pity on him and pardoned him. As soon as the words of the mother pardoning him came out of her lips, the son started reciting the forgotten Kalima *Tayyaba*, and died peacefully.

Such awe-inspiring incidents are really lessons for us. We must keep them in view while dealing with our parents, particularly mothers. In the presence of the above Quranic injunction and the Hadith coupled with the incident, now there is no need to say anything more.

The daughters-in-law should not forget that they too have children, and shall be in the same predicament one day. They are also future

mothers-in-laws. If they do not like to deviate from
their way which is based on prejudices, false pride,
hatred and disrespect for the elders, they should also
be prepared to be paid back in the same coin. God is
not related to anybody. He has prescribed certain
rules and regulations for us to bring them into practice.
He shall be with those who obey Him. We should not
be disappointed in the face of difficulties.

In *Surah Hud, Ayat No. 9*, there are lines that tell
us about the human tendency to forget even God if he
attains even minimal success in life. *Verse No. 11* of
the same Surah says that the persons who have been
bestowed upon by the Almighty or have created in
themselves a habit of having patience and fortitude,
are exempt from this phenomenon. As a matter of fact
both the position i.e. forgetting of God in happiness,
or becoming disappointed in misery, both are suicidal.
The proper way of a man is, therefore to be steadfast
under all circumstances. *Maulana Abul Kalam Azad*
while expounding verse No.83 of Surah Israil in his
Tarjuman-ul-Quran, has said that like in the
materialistic world the same principle works in the
spiritual world too. The virtuous (Muttaqi) people, by
a mere touch of pride on account of their virtues in
them, and the transgressor, by falling prey to a
bit of disappointment on account of his sins virtually
invite their death. In both the conditions both of them

are losers. Conversely, those, who guard themselves against both are really gainers. It is thus established that we must be steadfast under all circumstances.

9

BIRTH CONTROL

Hadrat Jaber has said that once a man approached the Holy Prophet (Peace be upon him and his progeny) and revealed:

"I have a slave girl. I cohabit with her in addition to getting the house-hold work done from her. I am afraid if she is conceived, there is nobody to do my work."

In this way, he sought the permission of the Holy Prophet (Peace be on him and his progeny) for taking some precaution against her being conceived.

The Holy Prophet (Peace be on him and his progeny) replied:

"You may take precaution if you like, but remember! what God wills it has to happen."

The man concerned returned to his home. After some time he again came and said that the slave girl had conceived. The Holy Prophet (Peace be on him and his progeny) replied:-

"I had forewarned you that God does what He wishes". Some people in those days used to practise "Azal".

Azal is an Arabic word, which means withdrawing the male organ from the vagina before, or at the time of discharge. In technical sense it implied unproductive sexual intercourse. (coitus Interruptus). What the Holy Prophet (Peace be on him and his progeny) wanted to convey was that the sexual act is a natural process of conception but every such act does not inevitably create children. It is just a mere chance that one of the strongest sperms springs out and gets entry into the womb, and a woman conceives.. It is certainly beyond one's control. If we study the process of birth biologically, we will find that like all other phenomenon of nature, the final dispensation is in the hands of the Almighty Lord. The scientists are of the opinion that one discharge sprouts innumerable sperms. The women of the whole world can be conceived with one such emission. All the sperms except one, the strongest of all, go waste. The theory of the 'survival of the fittest' comes into practice.

The use of contraceptive is injurious to health, Dr. Amand Routh who before the commission of enquiry, has revealed; "I have no doubt that prevention of maternity by artificial method invariably produces physical, mental and perhaps moral harm to those who resort to it. There is no sure method of birth control except operation."

Besides, we think that the drops of semen beget children, it is also not correct. It is often seen that the semen has no potentiality. The procreation depends only upon the will of God, and not on Azal, or the use of contraceptive, but God has made the semen a means of procreation. God is All-Powerful.

> Narrated Abu Sa-Ad Alkhudri : "We got female captives in the war booty and we used to do coitus interruptus with them. We asked the Allah's Prophet (Peace be on him and his progeny) about it and he said:
>
> 'Do you really do that? repeating the same question thrice.
>
> 'There is no soul that is destined to exist, but will come into existence, till the day of resurrection.'
>
> (Bukhari)

Sa'ad Abu Waqqas (Allah be pleased with him) reported that a person come to Allah's Prophet (Peace be on him and his progeny) said :

"I do Azal with my wife."

Allah's Apostle (Peace be on him and his progeny) said."

Why do you do so?"

The person replied: "I fear harm to her infant child."

The Prophet (Peace be on him and his progeny) replied:

"If it were harmful it would have harmed the Persians and the Greeks by now."

(Muslim)

The people think that lactation period is exception to cohabition, but it is not correct. Conversely, the ladies have an intense sexual appetite during such periods, but due to their being shy in nature, do not disclose it. We should not be oblivious to this aspect also.

Hadrat Abu Sayeed has said that the Holy Prophet (Peace be on him and his progeny) in reply to a question regarding Azal has said :

"Every drop of semen has no power of creation. It is the will of God, which controls the children creation".

(Muslim)

Judama, daughter of *Wahab Al-Asadiyya* (Allah be pleased with her) reported that she heard *Allah's Messenger* saying;

"I intend to prohibit cohabitation with a suckling woman, until I considered that the Romans and the Persians do it without any injury being caused to their children."

Replying to a question regarding Azal, the Holy Prophet (Peace be on him and his progeny) once said:

"Azal is the secret way of burying alive."

The words 'burying alive' allude to the practice of pre-Islam Arabs of burying female children alive either from fear of hunger or disgrace.

10

SODOMY IN THE EYES

OF GOD

Jaber (Allah be pleased with him) has reported that the Holy Prophet (Peace be on him and his progeny) saying that the Jews used to say:

> "When a man has intercourse with his wife through the vagina, but being on her back, the child will have squint, so the verse came down."

> 'Your wifes are your tilth: go them unto your tilth as you may desire."

> (Tirmidhi)

This *Hadith* has been reported on the authority of Jabar, there is an addition of the words

> "If he likes he may have intercourse being on her back or in front of her, but it would be through one opening (Vagina).

Contrary to popular ideas Islam is the only religion which candidly discusses sexual attitudes. There is nothing profane in Islam if some important aspect of life is taught to the public. Every act is sacred and can contribute to religious piety provided it is done according to the *Command of Allah* and with full sense of moral responsibility. The Muslims have been exhorted to supplicate before the Lord even at the time of sexual intercourse, when men is about to be swayed by the urge of flesh.

The *Holy Quran* contains directions for the physical as well as moral and spiritual welfare of man and it deals with the most delicate questions in a language the like of which cannot be found in any human literature. Here the woman is compared to "tilth" and man has been instructed to sow seed in the tilth with the same sense of responsibility with which the cultivator cultivates the land. This also implies that this act of sexual intercourse be directed to some fruitful results, and *should not be a vain delight.* It strikes at the very root of the filthy idea of unnatural offence since intercourse from the rear is never productive.

The conjugal act is the right of husband, and the woman cannot deny it without a valid and resonable cause. If it is refused against the wishes of the husband, there is every likelihood of his going astrayed, resorting to immoral practices for his sexual satisfaction. The woman too has similar right over her husband.

The Prophet (Peace be on him and his progeny) said:

> "God is not ashamed of allowing you intercourse with your wives through anus, if it has not been benefit to you."

(Ahmed)

Shariah has declared sodomy (either with male or female) "Haram" (Prohibited). Its doer is charged with inequity. It is equal to eating the flesh of kite, crow, vulture and swine.

The Prophet (Peace be on him and his progeny) said:

"Who does sexual intercourse through anus, is heretic."

Besides, from the medical point of view also it is injurious to man and woman both. The man becomes incapaciated to satisfy his wife. It is a slow-poisoning and plays havoc with the health of both. The woman, being subdued to her sexual passion, and finding her husband unable to satisfy her, may commit adultery which is a sin, and crime against the society.

The Prophet (Peace be on him and his progeny) on some other occassion has said :

"The sodomites and the persons, who indulge in intercourse with wife from the anus, are kept away from the grace of God."

(Sharah Al-Nisa)

The Prophet (Peace be on him and his progeny) has once said :

"God hates the sodomites, and those who quench their lust with their wives from back-side."

(Tirmidhi)

11

AMOUNT OF DOWER

Hadrath Abi Salma told that it has been reported by *Hadrath Aisha* that the dower of the Holy Prophet (Peace be on him and his progeny) was only 500 Dirhams - equal to Rs. 131.25 approximately.

(Muslim)

Just see the dower of the Holy Prophet (Peace be on him and his progeny) and compare it with the dower of today. Is there any commensuration between the two? Not at all. The only ground in favour of the fixation of huge amount of dower is inflation, which was alien to the people of yester years. No doubt, Rs, 131.25 of that period cannot be compared to an equal amount of today in value, but we must see the substance of the dower. What is the rationale behind it? It is equal to imposition of restriction, or checks on the husbands against taking liberty of having conjugal relations with his wife. The husband has to pay certain amount for access to her. The wife can claim prompt dowry from the husband immediately, before the consummation of marriage. Why do people prefer to settle huge amounts of dower for their daughters ? The only answer is that they had no faith in God, and do not think Him a sustainer. They believe that fixation of huge amount of dower would be a guarantee of sustenance to their daughters, but that is not true. The fixation of huge amount of dower may be a check on the husband but is not a guarantee of his conduct that he shall continue to keep the wife with him under compulsion, or with a fear of paying the dower to her in case he leaves her. It is often seen that the amount of dower is not realisable even from the property of the husband, if the mutual relations inter se are snapped. Conversely, husbands under no circumstances leave their wives even after paying dower to them. The real thing which counts in marital matter is mutual love, intense sense of sacrifice, blind faith in each other, sincerity, and nothing else.

The Prophet (Peace be on him and his progeny) fixed the same amount of dower in the marriages of His daughters, except *Hadrath Fatima,* whose dower was only Rs. 150/- *Hadrath Omar Bin Khitab* has advised the *Ummah* not to fix huge amounts in dower.

He said: "If there was anything meritorious in it, the Holy Prophet (Peace be on him and his progeny) would have himself fixed huge amounts in his own marriages, or atleast in the marriages of his daughters."

(Tirmidhi & Ahmad)

Jaber reported that the Messenger of Allah (Peace be on him and his progeny) has said:

"Whosoever gives two handfuls of barely or dates as dower to his wife, he makes her lawful for him."

(Abu Daud)

This *Hadith* confirms the fixation of petty amounts of dower. Such paltry amount can be paid instantaneously. It can be called prompt dower. At the time of the first introduction with wife, according to some local customs, or we can call it, out of love or the gift of the first meeting, the bridegroom parts with some amount of money to his wife. Sometimes the amount is not paid in cash, but in the shape of some ornament, or some novelty, such as watch, or papers relating to some property etc, why a husband does not regard it as a part payment of dower. It is in consonance with *Shariah*. Our duty is to follow the actions of the Holy Prophet (Peace be on him and his progeny) and his companions in all walks of life. If we copy the *Hadiths* of the Prophet (Peace be on him and his progeny) & give a practical shape to its contents sincerely, there is no reason why our marriages do not become the fountains of domestic benedictions and blessings.

12

VALIMA (Marriage feast)

Ans Bin Ma'lik narrated that once *Abdul Rehman Bin Auf* came to Allah's Prophet (Peace be on him and his progeny). He had marks of Sufra (Yellow perfume) on his garb. Allah's prophet (Peace be on him and his progeny) asked him about the marks. *Abdul Rehman Bin Auf* told Him that he had married a woman from the Ansars. The Holy Prophet (Peace be on him and his progeny) asked: "How much Mehar did you pay her ?" He replied: " I paid gold equal to the weight of a date stone." Allah's Prophet (Peace be on him and his progeny) said to him : "Give a wedding feast, (Valima) even if with one sheep."

(Muttafiqa Eleh)

This Hadith tells us the importance of the fixations of a paltry amount as dower, and a marriage feast, but not too expensive. *Hadrat Abdul Rehman Auf* was a very close companion of the Holy Prophet (Peace be on him and his progeny) and he could not invite Him even, but the generous and broad-minded Prophet

(Peace be on him and his progeny) did not consider it as disgraceful. Though, he was rich, he never showed off his wealth and lived a life of simplicity.

Even the Prophet (Peace be on him and his progeny) did never give a lavish wedding feast on the occasion of any of his own marriages, when he married Zainab, the banquet was celebrated with the meat of one sheep only. Such was the noble character of the Holy Prophet (Peace be on him and his progeny).

The Prophet (Peace be on him and his progeny) stayed for three days at a place between *Khaibar* and *Madina*, and there he consummated his marriage with Safiya Bin Huyay. On this Ans Bin Ma'lik says :

> "Under the instructions of the Holy Prophet (Peace be on him and his progeny) I invited the people; to banquet, which consisted neither of meat, nor bread. The Prophet (Peace be on him and his progeny) ordered for the leather dining sheet to be spread and dates, dried yoghourt, and butter was provided over it, and that was the Valima of the Holy Prophet (Peace be on him and his progeny)."

Narrated Safiya Bin Shaiba:

> "The Holy Prophet (Peace be on him and his progeny) gave a banquet with

two madds of barely on marrying some
of his wives (1 madd is equal to 3/4
kilograms)

(Bukhari)

Ibne Umar (Allah be pleased with Him) reported
that Allah's Messenger (Peace be on him and his
progeny) said :-

"When anyone of you is invited to a
feast, he should attend it."

(Sahih Muslim)

Abu Huraira, used to say."

"The worst kind of food is the wedding
feast to which the rich are invited and the
poor are ignored. He, who does not
come to the feast, in fact, disobeys Allah
and His Messenger.

Imran Bin Hasin has reported that the Holy Prophet
(Peace be on him and his progeny) has prohibited us
from attending the invitation of a *Fasiq*.

(Mishkatha)

The foregoing Hadiths have highlighted the simple
living and high thinking of the Holy Prophet (Peace be
on him and his progeny) but we have no courage to
give practical shape to all whatever we have read in
the above lines. Are we ready to follow their footsteps
to assimilate the sublime ideas into our routine ? They

have shown us the practical path to tread on unsophisticated, simple and contended. But Alas ! we, the so-called followers of the Holy Prophet (Peace be on him and his progeny) seems to have forgotten the lofty ideas as laid down in the Holy Book.

Fasiq is a person, who breakes the laws of Allah deliberating Attending to his first will tantamount to honour the brazen faced law breaker.

13

POLYGAMY IN ISLAM

Generally a hue and cry is raised today when the people, without knowing the depth of the principles of polygamy, prevalent among the Muslims claim that this practice must be banned, as it is not in consonance with their own theories. They think that the Muslims are fortunate enough to have the privilege of having more than one wives for their 'delight' only, and are better than others so far as the enjoyment of flesh is concerned. Such people see only the one-sided picture of this aspect and forget its corresponding burdens, responsibilities and liabilities. No doubt, a Muslim can keep more than one wife at a time but in the present set up who does so ? Almost none. Even one wife and her allied burden is not easily bearable, not to talk of more than one. Besides, in the older days polygamy was not so easy and pleasurable as people think it to be. A husband was enjoined strictly to afford equal treatment to all his wives. I will discuss the issue at the appropriate place, and want to stress here only that those who blame the principle are not fully conversant with its obligations and duties. Before uttering something they should delve deep into the injunctions of the Holy Qur'an and the Holy Prophet (Peace be on him and his progeny) and should study the exact circumstances under which such privileges were allowed to be achieved. They should study the exact circumstances under which such privileges were allowed to be achieved. They should go deep into the rationale behind the principles. It is a matter of commonsense that the laws and rules are always formulated to remove certain pitfalls and anamolies. In the medieval period wars were frequent which took a heavy toll of human life. Therefore this system of polygamy helped to alleviate the sufferings of war widows and their children who would have otherwise perished. Furthermore, if a person finds that one woman is not sufficient for him, and he marries one more lady for him strictly in accordance with the rules prescribed by Islam, does he commit a sin? Is it better for him to go to brothels for his sexual satisfaction, which is against the tenets of spirituality, morality and health.

It is really a pity that there is so much of misconception regarding the concept of polygamy. People in other societies should realise that Islam came into the world to cleanse it of evils, & not to provide vain delights to its followers.

14

EQUAL TREATMENT TO WIVES

Ibney Abbas has said that at the time of his death, the Holy Prophet (Peace be on him and his progeny) had nine wives. Among all of them he divided each and everything, which He had with him, except one *Hadrath Sauda,* who, due to her old age, had surrendered her rights in favour of *Hadrath Aisha.*

Hadrath Sauda has established an example by her action of surrendering her rights in favour of her co-sharer, for the guidance of ladies of *Ummah.* Her action has enhanced the honour of the ladies in the eyes of womenfolk. This event teaches the ladies to be broad-minded. Their belief must be that God shall provide necessary sustenance to those, who, in order to please God, surrender their rights in favour of any of his friends, or co-sharer. Besides, there is a provision of revoking the surrendered right if the surrenderer so desires.

If a man has more than one wives, it is obligatory on him to do justice with each of them impartially. Their shares are equal. The husband should, with the consent of all, divide the period of his stay with each of them, i.e. one day, or one week with one wife. To keep more than one wives at one spot, in one night, is also not approved by the Holy Prophet (Peace be on him and his progeny) provided all of them agree to it. Similarly, intercourse with one wife in the presence of the other is also prohibited by the Holy Prophet (Peace be on him and his progeny) At the time of journey the husband may choose any of them to keep her with him, through the medium acceptable to all of them, or any other system, such as casting lots. Similarly, in affording provision for sustenances, clothing and lodging etc. the husband must be just and fair, and even-handed for all. If he does any irregularity, or shows carelessness or slackness on his part with any of the wives, even if she does not know, or does not see to it, he is answerable before God.

Name of the wives of the Holy Prophet (Peace be on him and his progeny)

(1) Hadrat Aisha   (2) Hadrat Hafsa

(3) Hadrat Umma Habiba   (4) Hadrat Sauda
Salma

(5) Hadrat Umma Salma,   (6) Hadrat Juwairya

(7) Hadrat Safiyya   (8) Hadrat Memuna

(9) Hadrat Zainab.

The jurists have consensus of opinion that the husband, who goes to one wife after *Maghrib* and to the other after *Isha* is answerable to God for spending less time with the second wife. He may spend more time with an ailing wife,. Similarly, if he himself is ill, he can call any of them, or all of them to the house of the wife with whom he is staying. *Hadrat Maulana Ashraf Ali Thanvi* is stated to have two wives. One eyewitness has narrated that he had a weighing scale fixed in the ceiling of his house and he used to divide everything in it for distribution equally to both of them. He used to stay with each of them and used to apportion his earnings in three parts, two-thirds for both the wives, and one-third for his own use, which he spent in providing boarding and lodging to the orphans and needy students. Despite much equitable distribution, he begged God, to forgive him, if, inadvertently, he failed to do justice to either of them. He generally advised the people not to keep more than one wive, as it is a very hazardous task and has prescribed one exception to this general rule of having one wife only, and that is the wife's incapacity of begetting children or any other reason beyond his control. However, the imparting of justice to each of them is of prime importance under all circumstances. There is no escape for husband from it whatsoever.

Maghrib Prayer is offered immediately after sunset, and Isha prayer in the night.

Abdul Rehman reported that when Allah's Messenger (Peace be on him and his progeny) married Hadrath Umma Salme (Allah be pleased with her) he visited her, and when he intended to come out, she caught hold of His cloth, whereupon the Allah's Messenger (Peace be on him and his progeny) said:-

> "If you desire, I can extend the time of my stay with you, but then I shall have to calculate the time of my stay with you and shall have to spend an equal time with each of the other wives."

After marrying a virgin girl, the Holy Prophet (Peace be on him and his progeny) has said that a husband may stay with her for a longer period of time than he does with others.

Narrated Al Qasim : Hadrath Aisha said :

> "Whenever the Prophet (Peace be on him and his progeny) intended to go on a journey, he drew lots among his wives so as to take one of them along with him. During one of his journeys the lot was drawn in favour of me and Hafsa."

(Bukhari & Muslim)

Hadrath Aisha said that the Holy Prophet (Peace be on him and his progeny) used to distribute each to distribute each of his ability and capacity, and then used to pray God to forgive him if any excess has been done unintentionally with any of them.

(Tirmidhi, Ibne Maja & Nisai)

The pre-requisite for a husband, who has more than one wife, is to do justice to all of them impartially. He will have to be remarkably meticulous. Even the slightest negligence on his part may render him answerable in the court of Allah, who knows well what wrong a person has done, in which manner, and to what extent. The institution of having many wives is approved by Islamic laws, but it has not been encouraged, as is evident from the restrictions imposed by the Holy Prophet (Peace be on him and his progeny) upon the husband to treat all wives equitably, and held him responsible even for a minor dereliction of his duties towards any of them.

Aisha narrated that during his fatal ailment, Allah's Apostle used to ask his wives, "Where shall I stay tomorrow"? He was looking forward to Aisha's turn. So all his wives allowed Him to stay where he wished, and he stayed at *Aisha's house* till he breathed his last. *Aisha* added :

> "He died on the day of my usual turn at my house. Allah took unto him while His head was between my chest and my neck and His saliva was mixed with my saliva."   (Bukhari)

The Holy Prophet (Peace be on him and his progeny) had tremendous love for *Hadrath Aisha* as she knew His likings and disliking well. During the period of one's illness it is but natural that the patient wants to keep by his side only that attendant, who is well-conversant with his various moods. On inquiring the same question again and again, all the wives grew anxious, and they anonymously allowed Him to stay with *Aisha.* The Prophet (Peace be on him and his progeny) is buried on the same spot in the same room of *Hadrath Aisha.* This episode further strengthens the theory of equitable justice with wives, even to the last breath. The Holy Prophet (Peace be on him and his progeny) did not want to injure that feelings of the wife, whose turn to stay with Him would have been skipped over. He did not disclose his desire to stay with *Aisha* to his wives, as he was afraid of the fact that they might take his desire as His Order, and feel offended on account of missing their turn to have company with Him. Besides, the Holy Prophet (Peace be on him and his progeny) knew well that His action shall be taken as footstep to tread on by His followers, who commit something repugnant to the spirit of Islam, taking this action as their guide. He only gave some subtle hints, which the astute ladies discerned thoroughly, Indirectly the consent of the ladies to give up their right to please the *Apostle of God* took place at juncture, where it was most necessary to come into being. This was one of the examples of commendable sense of justice of the Holy Prophet (Peace be on him and his progeny). It behoves us that we should not over-ride the right of a favourite over one's, who is not so dear to us, and the affected persons is necessary before giving any priority to him.

The Holy Prophet (Peace be on him and his progeny) said :

"It is not within your power to love equally all your wives. One may have more inclination towards some of them, but it is in your power to afford equal treatment to all."

The Holy Prophet (Peace be on him and his progeny) on some other occassion has said:-

"On the day of judgement, the person who fails to do justice with his two wives, shall be half-paralysed, and a proportionate punishment shall be awarded to those, who have more than two wives, and do not deal with them equitably. A wife from among the men of book too falls in the same category, in which a Muslim wife falls. All the wives have equal rights whether they are Muslims, or from the people of books."

15

INNATE NATURE OF WOMEN

> *Narrated Abu Huraira:* Allah's Apostle said:
>
> "The woman is like a rib; if you try to straighten her, it will break. So, if you want to get benefits from her, do so while she is as it is".
>
> (Mut-tafiqe Aley)

This *Hadith* deals with the nature of woman, which is not to be set in conformity with the desire of man. One must bear up with her by doing some adjustments in his own nature and behaviour. If the husband is not able to adjust himself, or tries to set her right, his own life may turn into Hell, and the marriage may come to an end. "Created from the rib" is a metaphorical expression which signifies the *stubbornness* generally found in the temperament of woman and that is due to their physique and psychological frame of mind. Women are physically weaker and, therefore, are unable to defend and protect themselves with their physical strength. Nature, by bestowing upon them two unique habits of stubbornness, and shyness, has equipped them for their own protection to safeguard their existence.

There is a difference in the temperament of man & women, which cannot be denied. Islam has given due regard to this difference and has exhorted us to treat woman kindly and tolerate the incompatibility of their temperaments. The rib is bent in its texture. It is not straight. It serves the purpose best for which it has been formed by God. The same is the case with women. She has been endowed with some peculiar qualities by physique and mind. She serves the purpose best in her present state. An endeavour to straighten her, or to make her conform to a man's views, or to make her perfectly compatible with a man's temperament, may flare up into chaos. It is, therefore, advisable, that the man should treat her affectionately.

The Prophet (Peace be on him and his progeny) said that there is no doubt that the woman is born from the rib of the man. She will never mend herself as you wish. If without trying to get her agree with you on all matters.

It is, thus in the light of these *Hadiths* established that obduracy is ingrained in women. Their moods are unpredictable. She may be happy at one moment, but annoyed at other. At one time she may be grateful and ungrateful at the other. At one time she may abide by you, and defy at the other. So, it is best for you to have patience and try to adjust yourself as you feel necessary.

Abu Huriara (Allah be pleased with him) reported Allah's Apostle (Peace be on him and his progeny) as saying:

> "A believer (man) should not hate a believing woman; if he dislikes one of her characteristics he may be pleased with another of her characteristic."

(Muslim)

This *Hadith* further confirms the bare foot of life that temperamental affinity between man and woman is nowhere found. If a husband feels irritated at the commission of certain act done by her, he may feel happy at the same time with some other act done or not done by her. We must not forget that man and woman are like two wheels of a cart. Each is incomplete without the other. Neither wheel alone is able to haul the cart. If the wife has some minus points, she is bound to have some plus points also. One must search for plus points in her, and lead a worthwhile life by appreciating her specific virtues. He must have patience and should not lose the temper on the short-comings of the wife so frequently. It is better if we ask her to adjust atleast to some possible extent, so that both could avoid a cat and dog life. In case she is not able to adjust herself, the husband should do so. Nobody, in this world is perfect except the *Messengers of God.* The man, who searches for a perfect fellow-being shall have to traverse alone on the path of life without any friend.

In this context, as we all know. Islam has endowed us with the gift of courtesy to make it our mentor and guide, and we must utilise it to the maximum instead of adopting some coercive or despotic methods for reforming the wife. It is generally seen that most husbands, instead of conveying their intention to her politely and humourously, burst into vituperation on occassion, when such unwanted comments are not at all necessary. Consequently, instead of reformation some sort of stubbornness begins to permeate between the husband and the wife. Besides, we must avoid direct reformatory speeches to her in the presence of all. We should adopt some indirect methods to reform her. The Quranic injuctions in this respect prefers to put a veil on the defects of others (including the wife's defects) rather than make them public, so that the defaulter does not face humiliation and irritation. *Hadrath Nizam Uddin Aulia*, the great *Sufi* in such matters says that the reformer should employ illustrations to convey his messages to the disgruntled one instead of calling her names. He further says that he should win all by his sweet tongue instead of showering bristling criticism on her. He

should respond to her with love instead o
create an atmosphere of friendship and in
the house. The defaulter must be cornered
her faults voluntarily. These tactics are in ⌐   ⌐y
with the Holy Quran, and therefore, are bound to bear
fruit for the entire world, and Muslims in particular.

Abudulla Bin-Zaman reported that the Messenger
of Allah (Peace be on him and his progeny) said:

> "None of you shall whip his wife like
> whipping of slaves, and afterwards
> cohabit with her at the end of the day."

> (Bukhari & Muslim)

How funny it seems out to be when the husband
batters the wife in the day, and persuades her to enjoy
sex with him during night. Can she forget the husband's
blows within such a short period? Such husbands are
certainly immodest. To avoid such humiliating
methods, we must not do anything repugnant,.

The Holy Prophet (Peace be on him and his
progeny) has stressed time and again that we must
lead a peaceful life with our wive's temper. So far as
the duties of the wife are concerned, it is said that the
ladies are not entrusted with the work of cooking food
for us by the Almighty. We are obliged to get such
works done from them. In the routine, if any corner for
criticism is left, no doubt, we should pin point it to her,

but should not make it a prestige issue and bully her for it. We can make our homes *Heaven of Peace*, if we have patience and perseverance. Regarding the ways of making our life pleasant one, Holy Prophet (Peace be on him and his progeny) has guided us a lot.

16

SENTIMENTS TO BE HONOURED

Hadrath Aisha had reported that she, being of a tender age, used to play with dolls alongwith her friends in her house. The advent of the Holy Prophet (Peace be on him and his progeny) in the house sometimes disturbed the show. He always asked her to resume her games in which she was busy, for the sake of her friends. This *Hadith* teaches us that we must honour the susceptibilities of the wives, as they are also human beings and have sentiments. Describing some other incident she has said that once a chivalrous show of spears was held by the Negroes in front of the house of the Prophet (Peace be on him and his progeny). She came to the door and started seeing it. The Holy Prophet (Peace be on him and his progeny) unfurled his bed sheet vertically in front of her and asked her to see the show from behind the hole created by *Him* between the bedsheet and his shoulder. He thus kept standing till she saw it to her full (This incident had occurred before the revelation of 'Ayat-e-Hijab').

The Prophet (Peace be on him and his progeny) used to please his wives in all possible manners. He was of the opinion that was the only way to gain the wife's confidence and establish good relations with her, on which the whole journey of life depends.

> Once Aisha narrated what the Allah's Prophet said to her: "I know when you are pleased with me, or angry with me." I enquired: "How do you know that ? "The Prophet replied (Peace be on him and his progeny) "when you are pleased with me, you say 'No'! by the Lord of Mohammed, and when you are angry with me you say No! by the Lord of Ibrahim."
>
> Thereupon I said : "Yes! (You are right) but by Allah O! Prophet of Allah, I leave nothing but uttering your name."
>
> (Muttafiqa Eleh)

It is, no doubt, correct that the petty fracases between the husband and the wife, do take place in every house, and the Holy Prophet (Peace be on him and his progeny) also did not find himself free from such trifles of routine nature. The point here to remember is that with how much fortitude the Holy Prophet (Peace be on him and his progeny) on such occasions faced or circumvented them.

Hadrat *Aisha* said that during the course of the

journey, out of joke, she happened to run in order to outpace the Holy Prophet (Peace be on him and his progeny) like that in a race, and outran him. After a little while she was tired and he outran her. "I had to run faster this time as you had left me behind previously." The Holy Prophet (Peace be on him and his progeny) remarked."

(Abu Daud)

These Hadiths highlight the informal and unhesitant behaviourial aspect of life of the Holy Prophet (Peace be on him and his progeny) with his wives. How frank and genial he had been with them can be guessed by these incidents. He has emphasised the need of mixing up with the wife and has thus proved that all the strings of estrangement should be broken.

On another occassion *Hadrath Aisha* said that after the crusade of *Batul Ya Hassin* the Holy Prophet came (pease be on him and his progency) to her house, and seeing the dolls kept on a niche enquired;

"What is this Aisha?"

"My dolls." I replied.

"And what is that?" pointing out to a toy the Holy Prophet (Peace be on him and his progeny) asked.

"This is a horse." I replied.

By chance the horse had a set of wings. The Prophet (Peace be on him and his progeny) enquired:

"Has the horse two wings?"

"The horse of *Hadrath Solomon* had a power to fly, wasn't so ? I improvised."

Listening to it the Holy Prophet (Peace be on him and his progeny) burst into laughter so loudly that His inner teeth were clearly visible.

This behaviour of the Holy Prophet (Peace be on him and his progeny) stresses the need to inculcate in us a habit of merry making in our houses, mixing up with our wives, participate in their traits and seeking interest in their affairs. The informal message of the Holy Prophet (Peace be on him and his progeny) sent by him through *His actions*, shall echo through the corridors of time to come. It shall create harmony in the discordant elements of society.

It is reported by *Hadrath Aisha* that the Prophet (Peace be on him and his progeny) once said:

"The best among you is the man, who treats his wife and children affectionately, and humanly. As I am the best among you, follow my action."

Hadrath Abu Huraira has related that the Prophet (Peace be on him and his progeny) had once said that the most faithful among the Muslims is the person, who has good habits and enviable character and deals fairly with every body, and with the wife particularly, as the latter belongs to the weaker sex.

Hadrath Laqiq said :

"Once I approached the Holy Prophet (Peace be on him and his progeny) and told him that the conduct of my wife is not bearable. She often quarrels with me, and showers bad name on me."

The Holy Prophet (Peace be on him and his progeny) replied."

"Why don't you divorce her ? Your arguments and the way of narration about your woes reveal that you are intolerant, and for such a man, it is better if you divorce her.:"

I replied : "She is the mother of my child. Besides, she has been living with me for such a long time. I don't like to divorce her".

"Try to admonish her courteously and through some refined way, but don't beat her." Replied the Holy Prophet (Peace be on him and his progeny)

(Abu Daud)

Hakeem Bin Muawiya (from his father) reported: I asked.

"O! Prophet of Allah! what rights a wife
has over her husband ?"

He said : "It is that you shall feed her
while feeding yourself; that you
shall clothe her when you clothe
yourself; that you shall not slap her
on the face, nor revile her, not
leave her alone except within the
house."

(Masnad, Ahmad & Iba Maja)

In *Fatwa-e-Qadi Khan,* it has been clearly said
that the husband can punish or beat his wife on any
one of the following grounds :-

1.   If the husband desires the wife to live squarely
        and smartly but she neither takes bath, nor
        puts on good clothes, and cleans her body,
        nor takes care of keeping the husband clean
        and smart. (Cleanliness of body, house and
        the total environment is of prime importance,
        according to the principles of Islam. The part
        played by the woman in achieving these
        goals is thus   bolstered by the above
        injunctions of the Shariah. This means that the
        ladies have to abide by these rules even these
        are enforced by the husband with a heavy
        hand.)

2.   If the husband wants sexual intercourse,

and the wife without any reasonable cause avoids it or prevents the husband from enjoying such obligatory amusements.

3.   If the wife, after the lapse of her period does not take bath, and does not clean herself.

4.   If the wife, except in the prescribed circumstances and prohibited period, is addicted of giving up Namaz."

Besides, if the character of the wife is not good or reliable atleast, the husband , in order to set her right, can beat her under the most compelling circumstances, provided all other methods of bringing her home have failed. The husband is accused of inequity if he harrasses the wife unnecessarily. His action is not approved if he beats the wife on trifles, such as cooking of untasty food, non-washing of clothes, mistreating other members of the family, by-passing the normal and equitable norms of the family in routine matters. She is dependent on him and has no recourse to any other person than her husband. If he too rejects or hates her, where will she go and whom will she call for help and who, in turn, will have their privilege to come to her rescue ? The Holy Prophet (Peace be on him and his progeny) says that the persons who abuses his wife, is disobedient, and seems flouting the Godly laws. His witness is not trust worthy in the court of Shariah. Performing Namaz behind such person is not allowed.

Hadrath Moavia Binul Hukum, a Companion of the Holy Prophet (Peace be on him and his progeny) has said that he had a slave girl, to whom he had entrusted the job of a shepherdess. Once she was a little inattentive towards the goats, in a forest between *Ohad* and *Jawania,* when a wolf killed a goat. The master, hearing this incident, trembled with rage. Despite his endeavour to restrain himself, he slapped the slave girl in the huff. He, no doubt, felt ashamed thereafter but with the feelings of compunction, took recourse to the Holy Prophet (Peace be on him and his progeny) and narrated to *Him* the whole story. The Holy Prophet (Peace be on him and his progeny) got annoyed with him, and accused him of cruelty. He sought the Prophet's advice in order to avoid the wrath of God as an after-effect. The Holy Prophet (Peace be on him and his progeny) reprimanded the Companion concerned had told him to produce the slave-girl. Consequently, the slave-girl was produced, from whom the Prophet (Peace be on him and his progeny) enquired: "Who am I?"

"Messenger of Allah." she replied. "Where is God, do you know." The Prophet (Peace be on him and his progeny) asked :

"In the Heavens, OH! Prophet of Allah! The slave-girl replied.

The Prophet (Peace be on him and his progeny) through this exercise he wanted to know if the girl was having a faith in God and His Prophet. He forthwith advised *Moavia* to manumit her. The Hadith highlights a few gems for the *Ummah.*

1. Do not belabour the slaves, particularly a lady.
2. Do not be much annoyed over any loss provided it has not been caused deliberately by the slaves, or inferiors. Be kind to them even if they are your bond-servants, and purchased item over whom you have absolute and authoritative rights.
3. Manumit the slaves to please the Almighty provided he is faithful to Allah and His Messenger and believers in the hereafter.
4. Try to please Allah under all circumstances howsoever stringent they may be.

If we give thoughtful consideration to the above cited occurrence, we can learn that the Prophet (Peace be on him and his progeny) viewed the beating of the slaves very scornfully. How can he tolerate if we beat our wives, who are not our purchased items like slaves, Their period of Iddat is less. Repetition of the word "TALAQ" only twice is sufficient to break ties with them. The examples which I am citing are pointers to the fact that in Islam wives are given tremendous respect. If someone does the contrary he cannot be called a true Muslim.

One *Hadith* says that the deeds of His followers are presented twice a week before the Holy Prophet (Peace be on him and his progeny). Whatever *His Ummah* does. He comes to know of it. Misdeeds of the *Ummah* sadden *Him.* This is our misfortune that we torment Him by our deeds, inaction, carelessness, and obduracy. We must shed this outlook, and mend ourselves in order to please *Him* by some meritorious act. The perpetrators of sins are duty-bound to offer sincere apology. It is necessary to mention here that the act of high-handedness and maltreatment of a husband meted out to his wife is the infringement of *"Haqqul Ibad".* and unless the wife forgives him, he is not saved from the sin through *Taubah* (Contribution) only.

---

1. The Arabic word *Taubah* means both "To return back' and "to turn to". When applied to men, it means that he has turned back from rebellion to submission and, when it is ascribed to Allah, it means that He has again turned with Compassion to the penitent person. (Maulana Mau-didi's "The meaning of the Qur'an")
2. Haqqul Ibad consist of some inescapable duties enforced by God.

17

DIVORCE

Talaq is an Arabic word. It literally means freeing the spouse from the bonds of marriage. Repetition of the word Talaq three times in one breath, snaps the marital ties. Talaq is an ancient institution, and Islam has a pride of improving its shape by including therein a right of divorce to man and woman both. Simultaneously, it has commended again and again not to dissolve marriages frequently, and to take recourse to divorce only as a last resort. The right of a wife to claim Talaq is recognized by the Holy Quran, which will be discussed at the proper place.

According to Mohammadan Law, a husband may divorce his wife whenever he desires, without assigning any reason, at his mere whim or caprice. He may do so by mere words, and no particular form of words is necessary. If the words used are expressed or well-understood as implying divorce, no proof of intention is required. If the words used are ambiguous, the intention of the user must be proved. A Talaq is valid even though pronounced under compulsion, or in jest, or in a state of voluntary intoxication.

According to the *Hanafi School of thought,* the intention is immaterial. Therefore, if the words of divorce are expressed the *Talaq* is valid, even if it is given in a state of voluntary intoxication.

Abdullah Bin Umar reported that he divorced his wife while she was under menstruation. Umar mentioned it to the Holy Prophet (Peace be on him and his progeny) who became enraged at it and said:

> "Tell him (Your son) to take her back and keep her till she becomes clean, and then menstruates and then becomes clean. If it appears to him to divorce her afterwards, let him divorce her while she is clean before he touches her. This is the period of waiting which Allah enjoins for the divorce of women."

The rationale behind this philosophical advice, is that one should not take any hasty decisions regarding divorce and repent afterwards. The Holy Prophet (Peace be on him and his progeny) has prescribed methods of divorce also. He has pin-pointed the answers of every question. He knew that divorce is a very critical problem, as the future of the whole generation depends over the maintenance of domestic bliss. People who are rash, wander about in search of the ways and means to retrieve the status quo, but what is done cannot be easily undone. It cannot be taken back like a striken arrow from the bow. To eschew such humiliating results, the Holy Prophet (Peace be on him and his progeny) has forbidden us to pronounce *Talaq* thrice at one moment, and not at all during the menstruation period. He has prescribed remedies which prevents one from being impulsive and not utter *Talaq* during his wife's period.

He has directed us to pronounce only one Talaq at one moment, and that too in the period of wife's piety, and prohibited us from sexual intercourse till the period of her menstruation. During the span of about more than three months, the husband may take more serious decision about his future' either to break or to maintain ties with her. Such a divorce is very rational in its nature and is called "*AHSAN*" or a simple divorce.

The second kind of Talaq is called "*HASAN*". After pronouncement of *Talaq* twice consecutively, at one moment, the marriage is dissolved. To re-establish the marital ties after such pronouncement, the performance of the whole procedure of *Nikah* is required again. The husband may allow her to become his wife after the second *Nikah* with her.

The last kind of divorce is very drastic and

unsympathetic. It is called *"TALAQ-E-BIDAT."* Pronouncement of Talaq three times at one moment, severs all long-standing relations with her till *Halala* is done to re-unite the ties.

The *Halala* is a real test of one's patience. In order to re-marry the former husband, according to Shariah, the woman has to marry some other man after the period of Iddat of three months. She will again have to take divorce from the second husband, and after passing a period of three months as *Iddat* she may re-marry her former husband. It is also a compulsory ingredient of *Halala* that the second husband, or we can call him an intermediary husband too, should do sexual intercourse with her. Such nerve-breaking and sniggering procedure of re-marriage coupled with such disgraceful smirking, and humiliating outcome of one's hasty step, as a matter of fact, is a kind of punishment for both the imprudent participants of the ugly drama. For a man it is equal to licking up his own filth like a dog. No more severe punishment than the act of *Halala* with some other man, ending on divorce afresh and re-marrying with former husband again, can be there for a decorous and modest husband. A similar punishment through the *Halala* is awarded by the *Shariah* to a woman too. She has to coax and cajole her intermediary husband, at the cost of shedding the glorious past memories of her amorous moments enjoyed by her with the ex-husband. She has to suppress forcefully her innerself somehow or the other to compromise with the new circumstances, which may demand major adjustments also, although she feels herself crippled and finds no joy in living except ruminating over the past. The former husband too has similarly to brook the pangs of snatching of his wife from him due to his taking a hasty step. He has to see helplessly and not to lament at all, in the face of appalling scene of *establishing* conjugal relations of his once beloved wife with some other man. Similarly, the woman has to shower all privileges upon her new and temporary husband including his free access to sexual intercourse. What kind of man is, who tolerates such liaison of his wife with some other man. After both are humiliated, then they can once again revert back to their former status. People normally enjoy such juicy incidents. Now the question comes up whether such husbands are hard hearted. It is not so. They have just been brazen and careless and are paying for it.

On the other hand such incidents are sometimes generated also by the carelessness of the wife also. Had she at the moment of *Talaq* been a little agile, courageous, and alert, she could have stopped the husband from embarking upon divorce by gagging his mouth with her hands, per force. She could have avoided the hapless mishappening, which begets such pathetic results. Such could have saved the

husband from being so demented through her polished
and refined attitude towards her requirements. It
was certainly better if she could have kept the family-
fracas confined to verbal salves, and got them solved.
The pangs of misunderstanding, which often prepare
fertile soil for the weed of hatred, mistrust, or defiance
to grow and thrive, could have been cleared by
mutual endeavour, patience and perseverance. The
circumstances leading to *Talaq* could have been
avoided. Mutual taunting, and recriminations, can be
assuaged at first and crushed finally by the intervention
of some sincere superior in the family. If no checks on
the rash acts of the parties are kept, society will jeer
at the perpetrators of *Islam* instead of alleviating
agony of the disgruntled led, about which the *Holy
Qur'an* has commended:

> "If you fear a breach between the two,
> appoint arbitrator each from the family of
> husband and wife. If they both desire
> agreement, Allah will effect harmony
> between them. Surely, Allah is Ever
> knowing and Aware."

(4.35)

Is undergoing *Halala* not a punishment to both the
parties? Is it not a fierce slap on the face of both of
them? Is it not the test of one's patience, as I have
already said? Do not such persons demean

themselves? God may save us from such disgracing and mortifying acts. "Amin"

Mahmud Bin Labeed, reported that the Messenger of Allah (Peace be on him and his progeny) was once informed about a man, who gave three Talaqs at one moment to his wife. Then He (Peace be on him and his progeny) got up enraged and said:

> "Is the Book of Almighty (The Holy Quran) being made a plaything while I am still among you."

(Nisai)

One of the Companions of the Holy Prophet (Peace be on him and his progeny) discerned the surging sentiments in the heart of the Holy Prophet (Peace be on him and his progeny) and enquired: "Oh! Allah's Prophet (Peace be on him and his progeny) should I slay such disobedient.?"

This Hadith reflects the implied intention of the orders of the Holy Prophet (Peace be on him and his progeny) regarding the husbands, who pronounce three Talaqs at a time in a huff. In view of Imam Abu Hanifa, three consecutive Talaqs at one moment outcast the husband from the Ummah.

The venture of a Muslim to go haywire courtesy to the Shariah Rules, lands him nowhere. He is reprobate, and away from the grace of God. Those, who are inattentive to such calls of the Prophet (Peace be on him and his progeny) or Quran, must take lesson from the above quoted incidents taking place in and around us.

Hadrath Abdullah Bin Omar has reported that the Holy Prophet (Peace be on him and his progeny) said:

> "The most detestable of lawful things near Allah is divorce."

(Abu Daud)

The Holy Prophet (Peace be on him and his progeny) has denounced the act of Talaq and compared it to saying of "Namaz performed" but undoubtedly, it is impure and not God-propitiating in its real sense.

Moaz Bin Jabal reported: The Messenger of Allah (Peace be on him and his progeny) said to me:

> "O! Moaz! God created nothing on the face of the earth more dear to Him than emancipation of slaves and nothing more undesirable to Him than divorce."

(Mishkatha)

Hadrath Sheikh Ibne - Imam has also recorded in "Fateh-ul-Qader" that the divorce to a woman, who does not say "Namaz" or does not bear good character, is approved. In Fatwah-e-Qazi Khan, it is impressed that a "Namaz-shirking" woman deserves divorce, even at the cost of not paying her dower. From Abu Hafsa Bukhari, it is reported that in the eye of Allah, a person, who divorces his wife for her dereliction towards "*Namaz*", and being unable to pay her dower does not pay it, is better than a husband, who does not divorce his "Namaz-shirking" wife, and pays her dower.

In the light of the above *Hadiths* and the subsequent opinions of the Islamic Jurists, it is thus established that the *Namaz* is one of most important duties assigned by the Almighty to the *Ummah* to discharge properly, and sincerely. Dereliction towards *Namaz* howsoever paltry it may be, tantamount to inequity. We have, from time to time, been warned to adhere to it sincerely, so that in the eyes of *Allah* we are not downgraded, and our future generations do not suffer. "Namaz, as a matter of fact is the sustenance of one's soul, balm for his wounds, and panacea for his ills" but it is a pity that the husbands of today divorce their wives for the latter's temperamental non-adjustments with them, or for some other reasons but nobody comes forward to divorce his wife for non-saying of "Namaz."

The Holy Prophet (Peace be on him and his progeny) is reported to have said :

> "Three acts, even if done inadvertently, or even in joke, tantamount to their commission. (1) Nikah, (2) Divorce; and (3) Revocation of Talaq, (except Talaq-e-Bidat)."   (Rawah Tirmidhi)

Declaration of one's acceptance in the presence of atleast two free, sane major Muslim males, for the acceptance of a particular lady, unintentionally, or even in joke, tantamount to "*Nikah*". The act of pronouncement of divorce also takes effect even if the word "Talak" uttered in joke. So is the case with *revocation of Talaq.*

Hadrath Ali has narrated that the Holy Prophet (Peace be on him and his progeny) has exempted three categories of persons from application of the provisions of the above law. (1) Minor, (2) Fully or semi-concious, or a sleeping person until he awakes, and (3) Idiots or incapacitated.

Hadrath Aisha has reported that she had heard the Holy Prophet (Peace be on him and his progeny) saying "

"There is no divorce and emancipation of slaves by force."

Hadrath Imam Shafai has accepted this idea as it is but Imam Abu Hanifa, is of the opinion that Talaq, which is derived under compulsion, duress, or got forcefully announced is also complete and effective.

Divorce by mutual consent, in Islam, is called "*Khula*". It is with the concurrence of the wife. It signifies an agreement entered into for the purpose of dissolving the connubial connection in consideration of a compensation paid by the wife to her husband out of her property.

18

NASTY ASPERSIONS

Abdullah Yusuf Ali in "The Glorious Qur'an has expounded verse No.2 of Surah Nur, in the following words:

"Islam commands sex purity, for man & woman at all times - before marriage, during marriage, and after marriage, and after the dissolution of marriage. Those of illicit practices are shut out of the marriage circle of chaste men and women. It has prescribed very severe punishment for adultry and fornication."

Verse Number two:says:

"The woman and the Man
guilty of adultry or fornication,
Flog each of them
With hundred strips:
Let no compassion move you
In their cases, in a matter
Prescribed by God, if you believe

In God and the last day:
And let a party
Of the believers
Witness their punishment."

It has clearly been said that the punishment should be open, in order to be deterrent. Similarly for those persons who frame false charges against their chaste women, the Holy Qur'an says :-

"And those who launch
A charge against chaste women,
And produce not four witnesses
(To support their allegations)
Flog them with eighty strips;
And reject their evidence
Even after: for such men
Are wicked transgressors."

It means if anything is said against a woman's chastity it must be supported by evidence twice as strong as would ordinarily be required for business transaction or even in murder cases, i.e. four witness."

Narrated *Abu Huraira:*

"A man came to the Prophet (Peace be on him and his progeny) and said : 'O'! Prophet of Allah ! (Peace be on him and his progeny) a black child is born to my wife."

It means he doubted the chastity of his wife and sought the opinion of the Holy Prophet (Peace be on him and his progeny) before reaching a conclusion in the matter. The Prophet (Peace be on him and his progeny) asked him:

"Have you got camels?:"

The Man replied :"Yes". The Prophet (Peace be on him and his progeny) asked further: "Of what colour they are ?

The man replied: "Red."

The Prophet (Peace be on him and his progeny) again asked:

"Is there a grey one amongst them"?

He replied: "Yes"

The Prophet (Peace be on him and his progeny) enquired:

"From where comes that?"

The man replied : "It may be because of its heredity."

The Prophet (Peace be on him and his progeny) replied meekly:

"Your latest son may also be a black colour on account of his heredity."

(Bukhari & Muslim)

This Hadith instils in us a strong sense of bold and courageous outlook towards our wives. On the appearance of some unusual phenomenon we should not indict our wives of unchastity. We should not allow any rupture, doubt, or suspicion to stand in the way of our subtle relations with wives, unless contrary is proved. The possibility of some perverse streak in the character of the women, though cannot be totally ruled out, but such cases are very rare and every woman is not cheap, but exceptions are there, and one should not be completely impervious to this aspect also.

Hadrath Abu Huraira has reported that at the time of revelation of verses "*Mala-nat*" the Holy Prophet (Peace be on him and his progeny) said:

> "The woman, who commits adultery, and attributes her illegitimate child to her innocent husband is deprived of the entry into Heavens, and is kept off from the mercy of God. Similarly, a man, who indicts her wife of unchastity, and refuses to accept his own legitimate child as his own, will face the same dire consequences to which God has adverted to above."

(Rawah Abu Daud, & Nasai)

This *Hadith* forewarns the prepetrators of adultery to be ready to face the dire consequences. A very peculiar situation arises in a case where children demand their shares in the inheritance of their fathers, and the question arises, who is whose father ? The veil, which has hitherto shrouded in mystery the blackdeeds of our co-fellows, is pierced before the entire society. Is it not shameful for such deviated people ? Their children suffer endlessly. People laugh at them. Who is responsible for this. Can we answer? Of course! we ourselves, and our demented society where we do not fear Allah, and do not pay heed to the Quranic Orders, and the *Hadiths*, which left no room for doubts or clarifications in its meanings.

19

COURTESY AND VIRTUE

(1) Pride and Vanity

Hadrath Jaber bin Atik has reported that the Holy Prophet (Peace be on him and his progeny) has said:

"Pride and vanity are of two kinds:

(a) Desirable in the eyes of Allah

Pride over the victory in crusade after tough fighting and huge sacrifice, with the whole object of over-awing the enemy; and pride over distributing the obligatory alms to the needy and the poor to the maximum, and not to stop till the distributed the obligatory alms to the needy and the poor to the maximum, and not to stop till the distributed sum outnumbers the distributable amount, and the distributor still feels to do so more if he had more money: and (b) <u>Undesirable in the eyes of Allah</u>

Pride over one's origin or genesis has been discarded by the Holy Prophet (Peace be on him and his progeny) in his last sermon to the Ummah."

(2) Virtue

Nawwas Bin Sim'an Al-Ansari reported:

"I asked Allah's Messenger (Peace be on him and his progeny) about virtue and vice:"

He replied (Peace be on him and his progeny) replied:

"Virtue is a kind of disposition and vice is what rankles in your heart and that you disapprove of its being known to the people."

(Sahih Muslim)

(3) Relationship

God has enjoined upon us to maintain relationship which our forefathers had established with their friends or counterparts. Abdullah Bin Umar said that he had heard the Holy Prophet (Peace be on him and his progeny) saying:

"The finest act of goodness on the part of a son is to treat kindly the loved ones of his father:

(Sahih Muslim)

Jubair Bin Matin reported that his father narrated to him that Allah's Messenger (Peace be on him and his progeny) said:

"The severer of the tie of kinship would not get entry into paradise."

(Sahih Muslim)

Hadrath Abu Huraira *reported that a person said:*

"Allah's Messenger! I have relatives with whom I try to have close relationship, but they sever (relationship). I treat them well, but they treat me ill. I am sweet to them but they are harsh towards me."

Upon this the Holy Prophet (Peace be on him and his progeny)

"If it is so as you say, in fact, you throw hot ashes upon their faces, and there would always remain with you on behalf of Allah (An Angel to support you) who would keep you dominant over them so long as you adhere to this path (Path of righteousness)

(Sahih Muslim)

(4) Jealousy, Hatred and Hostility

Ans Bin Malik reported Allah's Messenger (Peace be on him and his progeny) as saying:

"Neither nurse mutual hatred, nor jealousy, nor enmity, and become fellow-brothers and servants

of Allah. It is not lawful for a Muslim that he should keep his relations estranged with his brother beyond three days."

Confirming the above Hadith, Hadrath Abu Ayyob Ansari reported Allah's Messenger (Peace be on him and his progeny) as saying:

"It is not permissible for a Muslim to have estranged relations with his brother beyond three nights, the one turning one way and the other turning the other way, when they meet; the better of the two is one, who is the first to give a greeting."

(Sahih Muslim)

(5) Suspicion and Oppression of fellow-brothers

Hadrath Abu Huraira reported Allah's Messenger (Peace be on him and his progeny) as saying :

"Avoid suspicion, for suspicion is the gravest lie in talk and do not be inquisitive about one another and do not spy upon one another and do not feel envy with the other, and nurse no malice, and nurse no aversion and hostility against one another, and be fellow-brothers and servants of Allah.

(Sahih Muslim)

Abu Dhar reported Allah's Messenger (Peace be on him and his progeny) as saying that He reported it from His Lord the Exalted and Glorious:

> "Verily I have made oppression unlawful for Me and for My servants too, so do not commit oppression."

(Sahih Muslim)

Jaber Bin Abdullah reported that Allah's Messenger (Peace be on him and his progeny) said:

> "Be on your guard against committing oppression, for oppression is a darkness on the Day of Resurrection and be on your guard against petty mindedness for petty mindedness destroys those, who were before you as it incites them to shed blood and make lawful what was unlawful for them."

(Sahih Muslim)

Noman Bin Bashir reported Allah's Messenger (Peace be on him and his progeny) as saying:

> "A believer is like a brick for another believer, the one supporting the other."

(Sahih Muslim)

(6) Abusing and Back-biting

Abu Huraira reported Allah's Messenger (Peace be on him and his progeny) as saying:

"When two persons indulge in burling (abuses) upon each other, it would be the first who would be the sinner so long as the oppressed does not transgress the limits."

(Sahih Muslim)

Abu Huraira reported Allah's Messenger (Peace be on him and his progeny) as saying:

"Do you know what is back-biting?"

The Companions replied:

"Allah and His Messenger (Peace be on him and his Progeny) only know the best."

Thereupon the Holy Prophet (Peace be on him and his Progeny) said:

"Back-biting implaies your talking about your brother in a manner, which he does not like."

It was said to Him (Peace be on him and his Progeny)

"What do you say if I actually find (that failing) in my brother, which I made a mention of?"

The Prophet (Peace be on him and his Progeny) said:

"If (that failing) is actually found (in him) what assert, you in fact back-bited, and if that is not

in him, it is a slander.

(Sahih Muslim)

(7) Forgiveness and Humility

Abu Huraira reported Allah's Messenger (Peace be on him and his Progeny) as saying:

"Charity does not in any way decrease the wealth and the servant, who forgives, Allah adds to his respect, and the one who shows humility, Allah elevates him in the estimation (of the people)"

(Sahih Muslim)

Abu Huraira reported Allah's Messenger (Peace be on him and his Progeny) as saying:

"The servant of Allah, who conceals the fault of others in this world, gets his own faults concealed on the day of resurrection by Allah."

(Sahih Muslim)

Hadrath Aisha reported from the Holy Prophet (Peace be on him and his Progeny) as saying:

"Verily in the eye of Allah, worst amongst the persons in rank on the day of Resurrection, is one whom the people abandon or desert out of fear of indecency."

(Sahih Muslim)

Jaber reported from the Messenger of Allah (Peace be on him and his progeny) as saying:

"He who is deprived of tenderly feelings is in fact deprived of good,"

(Sahih Muslim)

(7) Self Control Anger

Hadrath Abu Huraira reported from the Holy Prophet (Peace be on him and his progeny) as saying:

"The strong man is not one who wrestles well but the strong is one, who controls himself when he is in a fit of anger."

The Holy Prophet (Peace be on him and his progeny) said :

"The anger is the product of Devil, who is made of fire, Only water can extinguish the fire. Perform ablution if you feel anger."

(Abu Daud)

The Prophet (Peace be on him and his progeny) has advised :

"If you feel irritated while you are standing, sit down, anger will subside. In case so does not happen, lie down, it will vanish."

(Mushkatha)

(8) Sacrifice and Self restraints

Harire Bin Nom Abdullah has reported :

"I alongwith some other companions was sitting before the Holy Prophet (Peace be on him and his progeny) before the prayer of *Fajr*, when some sword-wielding persons, wrapped in rugs came. Major part of the body of each of them was bare. They belonged to the clan of *MUDHIR*. The Prophet (Peace be on him and his progeny) witnessing their poverty was moved, and his face turned pale. The Prophet (Peace be on him and his progeny) called *Hadrath Bilal* (God be pleased with him) and told him to make call for *FAJR prayer.* The Prophet (Peace be on him and his progeny) performed *Namaz* in congregation and sermonized the attendants. In *His* speech, (Peace be on him and his progeny) he recited the first *Ayat of Surah Nise,* and the first Ayat of the last section of *Surah Hasher,* and said :

'All of you should give away some *Dinar, Derhams*, clothes, palms and cereals in alms (In the name and for the sake of Allah)'

Hearing this, one of the Ansars immediately rushed to the Holy Prophet (Peace be on him and his progeny) and handed over to *Him* a bag full of money. Similarly, the others too copied his action, and within no time multiferous assortments were piled up there. Consequently the face of the Holy Prophet (Peace be on him and his progeny) gleaned with joy. *He* distributed everything among the new-comers and said :

'In Islam, a person, who takes first step towards

the establishments of a virtue, will get compensation by the Almighty. Similarly, the persons, who are prompted by his actions to copy him, will also be entitled to compensation by the Almighty. Thus the first-mentioned person shall get compensation on two grounds:

(i)   For establishing the virtue by his own self; and

(ii)   For leaving a track for others to treat on.'"

Hadrath Abdul Rehman Bin Abu Baker said:

"Once the Holy Prophet (Peace be on him and his progeny) saw some poor and hungry people. He advised all his companions to take one or two of them each (to feed) according to his capacity to afford. My father took three of them to my house and the Holy Prophet (Peace be on him and his progeny) took ten people with him (to feed)

(Bukhari and Muslim)

The Prophet (Peace be on him and his progeny) was the leader of the Muslims. If he himself had not taken ten people to his house to feed how could He expect the others to follow suit. The principle that emanate from this incident, is that the Leader or any other Responsible person should first take the initiative for any sacrifice and pave the way for others.

Hadrath Abu Huraira has reported that a person came to the Holy Prophet (Peace be on him and his progeny) and revealed that he was hungry. The Prophet (Peace be on him and his progeny) sent somebody to one of his wives to find out if there was something to eat. The Noble wife replied, 'Except some water there is nothing to eat in the house. 'The Prophet (Peace be on him and his progeny) sent the same man to the other wife for the same purpose. From there also the same answer was received. The Prophet (Peace be on him and his progeny) tried to get something for the stranger from all his wives, but nothing could be arranged. Being constrained, the Prophet (Peace be on him and his progeny) asked his companions if anybody could feed the stranger. One of the *Ansars* took the stranger to his house, who asked wife if there was something to feed the guest. The wife replied 'Something is there, but it is for the children, who are not present in the house.'

The *Noble Companion* advised his wife to fetch the eatables for the stranger, and said to her: " If the children ask for food, engage them in some other work, and make them sleep through patting on their backs gently. Blow out the light so that the stranger could not sense that he is alone on the dining sheet." After sometimes, the guest dined to his full, and the *hosts* slept unfed.

This is not the solitary example of sacrifice, self

control and restraint, established by the Noble Companions of the Holy Prophet. Islamic history is full of such instances without being fully influenced by the picture which the people depicted.

Hadrat Musaeb bin Omair, one of the companions of the Holy Prophet (Peace be on him and his progeny) was a very rich person and had everything that life could provide; the best horses to ride on; the best dresses to put on; the best buildings to live in. He lived very luxuriously before embracing Islam. Simultaneously, he knew well how wretchedly the Muslims lived but when he was offered Islamic faith, he did not hesitate to embrace it. He gave up everything and distributed his wealth among the poor. He migrated to Madina alongwith the Holy Prophet (Peace be on him and his progeny) and ultimately laid his life in the battle of Uhd for the sake of Islam. At the time of his death, he had nothing with him except a rug on his body, and that too, was in sufficient to cover him from head to feet, (after his death). If head was covered, the feat were bare, and vise versa. Ultimately, the Holy Prophet (Peace be on him and his progeny) covered his head with the rug and buried him in the same.

In Bukhari & Muslim both, a Hadith on the subject of changing one's origin or ancestral decendant is debarred from entering Paradise, on account of his act of cheating the others, which is a crime against the society as well. Presently it has become a fashion that the people, regardless of their origin, call themselves *Sayyad, Qureshi,* or *Ansari,* in order to get themselves adjusted in the society, or get their ulterior motives served, In the eyes of Islam this act of proselytism has no legs to stand on, not to talk of approval or disapproval of the Holy Prophet (Peace be on him and his progeny). The only thing which shall be scanned and adjudged on the day of resurrection is one's actions and intentions. The basic conception of Islam in this connection is contained in the last sermon of the Holy Prophet (Peace be on him and his progeny) which says:

> "God has removed from you the blemished of ignorance and the pride of birth. Now, there are only two classes of men those, who are righteous, and God-fearing; and those, who are wicked and sinful. An Arab has no superiority over a Non-Arab except of course that he excels the latter in piety."

Again on another occassion Hadrath (*Abu Zar* reported that the Messenger of Allah (Peace be on him and his progeny) said:

> "You are in no way better than the Red and Black except that you surpass them on account of piety."

> (Ahmad)

This *Hadith* has denounced the artificially created distinction between man and man. Islam recognizes that by birth everybody is equal in honour and respect. We are children of *Adam*, who was made of earth. All are equal. Pride of birth is insignificant, and smacks of ignorance. It is one's actions which counts. The world is full of allurements. It spoils the man and those fall prey to its temptations destined to be away from God and His Prophet (Peace be on him and his progeny).

> Narrated *Hadrath Aisha*: Hinda Bint Utba said :

> *"Oh ! Allah's Prophet ! Abu Sufyan (her husband) is a miser, and he does not give me sufficient money for me and my children. Can I take something from his money without his knowledge. ?"*

The Prophet (Peace be on him and his progeny) replied:

> *"Take what is sufficient for you and your children but the amount must be just and reasonable."*

> (Sahi Bukhari)

The Holy Quran in this respect behoves the husband, "Lodge them where you live, according to your means, and injure them not to straighten them. And if they are pregnant, spend on them until they lay their burden." (65.6) This Hadith and the injuction of the Holy Quran enjoins a husband to feel himself duty-bound to afford his wife and her children atleast so much money as is absolutely necessary for them, alongwith lodging, even if she is living separately from him, and he does not call her for any service, or otherwise. Such amount may be fixed as mutually agreed upon keeping in view the sources of the husband. In this connection a very important and worth mentioning aspect of *Islamic Law* has to be kept in view in arriving at some conclusion. In case, if either party, in order to avoid the provisions of the agreement, pleads to be poor and there is no reasonable man to decide the issue, the plea of the husband shall prevail provided the wife fails to prove to the contrary through some positive evidence. If the husband, on the other hand, is well-heeled, he shall have to administer all facilities for her including a maid-servant. In case the financial status of the husband changes from rags to riches or vise versa, due consideration must be given to the amount fixed for the wife accordingly.

There is one exception to the general rule of holding the husband responsible for the maintenance of his wife prescribed by the *Islamic Jurists.* If the wife, of her own volition, has shifted to her parents house against the wishes of her husband, he is not liable for her such expenses whatsoever. Similarly, after performing *Nikah*, if the girl is not brought to the husband's house due to her ailment, or otherwise, the husband is not responsible for her expenses, as are discussed above. Even a poor, husband, is not exempt from the responsibility of bringing up his family, He may give slip to other members of his family but not to the wife and her children.

The Holy Prophet (Peace be on him and his progeny) on one occassion, is stated to have said: "First priority over husband's property is that of wife and children. Others may get some out of it, provided it is spare, and more than the need of the wife and children, or according to the Rules of Shariah."

(Muslim).

The Prophet (Peace be on him and his progeny) has said :

> *"All of you are answerable for those, who are under your control : (Amir) Leader for the follower; Head of the family for support AND MAINTENANCE OF HIS WIFE AND CHILDREN; Wife for the upkeep and bringing up of children, and maintenance of full integrity and guarding her chastity against infidelity."*
>
> (Muslim & Bukhari)

20

EXTENT OF TAKING SERVICE FROM WIFE

The Apostle of Allah (Peace be on him and his progeny) is stated to have said :

> "Get services from your wife to a reasonable extent only. Do not overburden her and see that her health does not give away."
>
> (Rawah Muslim)

An *Hadith* in this respect has revealed that God, the *Almighty* imposes so much burden on a person, as he is able to bear. The Holy Prophet (Peace be on him and his progeny) has viewed that the same formula must be kept applicable in our houses also. We must remember that she is also made of the same material, of which we are, and she also feels tired after doing her work at home. We should not be unjust to woman while calling them for petty matters, specially when they are dining or taking rest after doing house-hold chart. It will be our selfishness if we have no human feelings for them. But, if they of their own accord, do something for us, we should be greatful to them.

Hadrath Abdulla Bin Osman has reported that the Holy Prophet (Peace be on him and his progeny) was very liberal to all in such matters even to the slaves. Once he said:

> "Refusal to boarding and lodging facilities to the wife, children, and the slaves by a man renders him sinful".

(Muslim)

Another *Hadith* in this context says:

> "Destroying the edibles and not giving them to the slaves pushes a man towards the Hell."

(Muslim)

In the preset set up, a fashion of joint-dining in a family is in vogue. This system is very good and is in accordance with the theory of Islam.

Hadrath Abu Masood Ansari has reported that once he was beating his slave. All of a sudden, from behind I heard:

"O Mosood !... Beware ! God is the mightiest. He has more control over you than you have on yourself."

I turned my face, and saw the Holy Prophet (Peace be on him and his progeny) standing behind me.

"O Prophet of Allah! I Manumit this slave I chipped in." It is better, otherwise you would have been pushed towards Hell." The Holy Prophet (Peace be on him and his progeny) replied.

(Muslim)

Hadrath Abu Amamata has reported that the Messenger of Allah (Peace be on him and his progeny) presented a slave to Hadrath Ali (Allah be pleased with him) and said; Don't beat him, as I have been prohibited from beating those, who say Namaz, and I have seen him doing so."

(Mishkat)

Hadrath Abu Baker (Allah be pleased with him) has reported that the Apostle of Allah (Peace be on him and his progeny) has advised the people not to beat those, who say Namaz, as they have better position in the eyes of Allah, due to their prayer.

(Mishkat)

Hadrath Abdulla Bin Omar has reported that a Companion came to the Holy Prophet (Peace be on him and his progeny) and said :

"O Messenger of Allah ! How many times shall we pardon a servant.,?"

The Holy Prophet (Peace be on him and his progeny) remained silent. The Companion repeated this question, but the Holy Prophet (Peace be on him and his progeny) again remained silent. When it was asked for the third time, the Holy Prophet (Peace be on him and his progeny) replied:

"Pardon him seventy times everyday."

(Abu Daud)

The Apostle of Allah (Peace be on him and his progeny) remained silent as he was waiting for some revelation on this issue which immediately descended on him. *Hadrath Abu Baker* has reported that the Messenger of Allah (Peace be on him and his progeny) said:

> "The doer of evil to the slave shall not be allowed to enter Paradise,"

Hadrath Sohel said that once an over-loaded and underfed camel was passing through a road, in front of the Holy Prophet (Peace be on him and his progeny) who being moved at the sight, took pity on the poor animal and said:

> "O bondsman of Allah ! Fear Allah, use the animals to the capacity, but do not overburden them. Feed them properly, and provide them rest before they are exhausted and tired."

(Abu Daud)

If the tender-hearted Prophet (Peace be on him and his progeny) can melt on seeing the helplessness of animals, can we imagine that He is not sensitive towards the human sufferings?

Hadrath Abdulla Bin Omar has reported that once a woman with an infant in her arms, came to the Holy Prophet (Peace be on him and his progeny) and said:

> "O Prophet of Allah ! I begotted and nourished this son. I faced all sorts of trials and hardships for him. His father has divorced me. Now, he wants to snatch my son from me kindly save me."

The Holy Prophet (Peace be on him and his progeny) replied :

> "Keep him till you re-marry some other man. The mother has an over-riding right over a son vis-a-vis a father."

> (Ahmad - Abu Daud)

Hadrath Abu Huraira has reported that once a woman came to the Holy Prophet (Peace be on him and his progeny) and said

> "O Prophet of Allah ! My husband has divorced me. I have an adult son, who looks after me. His father wants to take him from me. Kindly tell me what to do."

The Apostle of Allah (Peace be on him and his progeny) advised the youth :

> "You are adult, you may choose either parents to live with."

The youngmen preferred his mother. *Hadrath Abu Aiyoob* HAS REPORTED that his own ears the Holy Prophet (Peace be on him and his progeny) saying:

> "He, who causes estrangement and disunity between mother and her children, shall be separated from his own dears.

> (Tirmidhi)

Thus, it is evident that a mother should not be dispossessed of her child forcefully in the case of a divorce. In case the woman wilfully agrees to keep the child away from her, the children can be given to their father.

Sentiments in a huff, are always irrational and misguiding.

21

SOME HUMBLE SUGGESTIONS

Hitherto we have gone through the rights and duties of husband and wife with specific references to, and emphasis on the duties of a husband, as enshrined in the Holy Qur'an. It would be fair also to the subject if we also talked about the duties of woman and suggest something for them. The Holy Prophet (Peace be on him and his progeny) said:

> "The woman, who performs Namaz five times a day, does fasting during the whole month of Ramjan, guards her chastity and obeys her husband, can enter the Paradise through any of its gates."

This *Hadith* is very clear in its attributes, and calls for no comments. The Prophet (Peace be on him and his progeny) said:

> "The woman, who keeps her husband annoyed, is accursed in the eye of Allah".
>
> (Dalmi)

On some other occasion the Holy Prophet (Peace be on him and his progeny) said:

> "O woman ! Thy Heaven and Thy Hell is Thy Husband, His pleasure shall lead you into Heaven and displeasure into Hell."

As discussed earlier, there are several other *Hadiths* and injunctions of the Holy Quran determining the superiority of the husband over the wife, as she is biologically incapable of facing and withstanding the world in comparison to her husband. This state of affairs refers to the existence of an infallible to sincere relation between them an unshakable faith and infinite love and affection containing desires for sacrifice for each other till the last breath, which, if once created, will produce emotionally a well-knit atmosphere for mutual goodwill and respect for both of them. The above-quoted *Hadiths* are warnings to those women, who treat their husbands disgracefully, and take them as their servants, or merely a money-making machines. They do not care for the latters' usual bare necessities and requirements, such as serving (or getting served) the breakfast, lunch or dinner etc. at the proper time as desired by him. They keep their husbands entangled in their own whims, and fancies and are oblivious to his desires and wishes and look upon husbands and their own whims and fancies and are oblivious to his desires and wishes and look upon their husbands as their inferiors. In the light of the above *Hadiths* is it not obligatory on such women to mend their ways? The Holy Prophet (Peace be on him and his progeny) had once said:

> "If prostration to anybody other than God would have been allowed, I would have asked the wife to prostrate before her husband."

The Holy Prophet (Peace be on him and his progeny) would have brought the *Husband at par with God,* if the prostration to somebody else would have been allowed by the *Shariah*, as discussed earlier. What more can be said in regard to the importance and the definite status of the husband in the eye of the *Creater.* The main emphasis laid in such Hadiths is the recognition of his superior status. If both of them (Husband and wife) stick to their rightful position and jurisdictions, as prescribed by the *Holy Quran,* will not *Paradise* descend on earth for the *Ummah*?

On the basis of general experience and vast studies a few hints for the guidance of the ladies are given here, granted that in every educated family the ladies are well conversant with them, and the only need for their emphasis here is to remind them of which they have either forgotten or forsaken due to some carelessness or being too busy in their routine matters, with the expectation that the misgivings in the family matters, which often spoil the congenial atmosphere of a sweet home, will be warded off.

1. Keep in mind that the mutual relations with your husband depend on the mutual good-will, faith and love for each other as has already been discussed earlier. Once relations are strained they are not easily patched up. It is, therefore, necessary not to allow bitterness to exist in the family. Obey your husband to please the Almighty in the first instance, and to win him for ever in the other. Besides, when you know that you are with him for ever, and no escape, except divorce or death, is possible it is better to live peacefully instead of pushing the two lives into Hell by making adjustments with him from time to time

2. Avoid unnecessary altercating. Refrain from chipping in harshly when he is uttering something, even if he says something repugnant to your views or wishes. Adjust yourself patiently and wait for your turn to make him agree to you after sometime - when he is cool.

3. Avoid harshness in conversation, even if there has been a quarrel.

4. Do not ask for more money even for your household expenses. Do not compel him to do something beyond his capacity, capability, and means, Cut your coat according to cloth.

5.   Do not insist on purchasing anything which he neither is able to afford nor likes to buy. The wife loses her importance or has to cut a sorry figure if she is in the habit of putting forward her demands before him frequently.

6.   Do not complain about your penury, as nobody shall help you, rather people tease you again and again by reminding their favours once done to you. Your husband may feel offended for your defaming him because of such transitory impulses. Do not forget that our anscestors were of the view that *'worldliness is an unforseen calamity.'*

7.   Do not condemn the choice of your husband, even if it is not appreciated by you. But if he, of his own accord, brings something for you, accept it happily, so that he may feel pride in having a wife of his temperament and will shower much affection on you.

8.   Do not exacerbate his mood if he ever loses his temper. It is better to be silent for the time being atleast. You may explain your views later on to make him amenable and in conformity with you.

9.   If you have committed any mistake, admit it forthwith unhesitatingly. In the view of the Holy

Prophet (Peace be on him and his progeny) *Confession of an error is a great virtue."* Be critical of your own shortcomings.

10. Do not take service from him unless it has become absolutely necessary, such as during the period of your illness etc.

11. Do not search his pocket without his knowledge or permission.

12. Respect your father-in-law or mother-in-law etc. so that your husband may feel that you possess high moral virtue and know how to respect your elders. Be very mature and meticulous in such matters, and do not them lightly.

The biggest virtue of human being is politeness and courtesy which costs nothing, and augments your magnanimity and broad-mindedness instead. Every sincere woman is expected to possess such qualitites for gaining all round appreciation. There is no husband on earth who does not like to live peacefully in his family. As a wife, mere sweetness of your tongue will win him. Life is not a bed of roses, and one has to sacrifice something in order to achieve one's goal. It is generally seen that intelligent wives, through a little trick and refined manners, make their husbands love them more howsoever Devilish the latter may be.

13.   Treat his elders as your own. Love them as he loves. Consequently, love will begget love, and your love will be reciprocated.

14.   Do not hesitate in doing household work. Bring yourself at par with other members of the family by and by, so far as this field is concerned. If there is any maid-servant in the house treat her too affectionately. She will also give you due respect in the family. Being a new entrant in the family (if you are so) the new comer is showered comparatively more affection. The people may have high hopes from her. Do not allow such affection be lessened. Take the full advantage of the opportunity. Win all with your humorous and pleasing manners and courtesy.

15.   Do not speak much. First think and then speak. Live smartly within the limits of your financial status. Wear matching clothes. Do not run after much make up, if your husband or other members of your family do not like it. It is also not out of place to mention here that the indiscreet use of make-up spoils the face. Do not roam about unabashingly or unhesitatingly. Do not mix up with strangers

exhorted to learn what they lack and give up what they wrongly posses. They should not be treated ironically or despotically, but should be encouraged to be generous, humorous, and broad-minded. They must be made able to realise that there is some superior power to look after them and to watch their activities, (such as father). The children must be made informal in their behavior. Some moral booster stories of the heroic deeds of their forefathers must be related to them so that they may also like to become great. They should not be prevented from paying, but be directed to play strictly in accordance with some specific norms so that they may be strict disciplinarians while playing. It goes without saying that the playing is the field from where a child learns dicipline. They should not be allowed to waste money and edangering their health by nibbling here and there. Appreciate their good habits and goods deeds, and make them habitual of doing some exercise in the morning. Their necessities must be meted out. No sense of inferiority be allowed to over-power them. They must be taught to take an objective view of the situation without an intervention of sentiments whatsoever. They must be enforced to realise that the decisions taken by a person while subdued to sentiments or in a huff, are always irrational and misguiding.